LOVE NEVER FAILS

LOVE NEVER FAILS

DELIVERING JESUS' LOVE TO YOUR ADULT CHILDREN

Jeffrey Cranford & Jeff Hopper

LINKS PLAYERS PUBLISHING
A ministry of Links Players International
La Quinta, California

LOVE NEVER FAILS

To our parents,
who have persevered in faith
even when we have presented them their faith's greatest test

To our children,
for whom we want nothing more and nothing less
than a life given to Jesus

TABLE OF CONTENTS

Now adults, these children had fulfilled the horrifying words of Harry Chapin's "Cat's in the Cradle." They had mimicked their parents in the pursuit of lesser things. They had no interest in God.

FOR THOSE WHO GRIEVE
||||||||||||||||||||||||||||||||||||||||||||||||||||||||||||

THOUGH MORE THAN ten years have passed since I heard the words spoken, they have remained fresh in my mind and heavy on my heart.

Our group had assembled in the mountains of North Carolina—about twenty men, playing golf, eating well, talking seriously. I was the invited guest from across the country, so I didn't know any of them when I arrived. They were nearly all businessmen, or men whose hope it was to minister to businessmen, to get them to think about things that don't usually come up around the conference table at the office or the card table at the club. Big things. Deep things. God things.

Among them was a man whose family is well-known in the South. They have made important contributions not only in business, but also in politics and education. They are people of influence. The man was in his fifties, I'd say, and his own actions—which included alcoholism and reckless spending— had led him to a point of crisis in his life. When he asked those who seemed to have their lives together, he found that what he needed was the grace of Jesus. God's offer of salvation is no secret to American Southerners, where tent revivals and Gospel-shouting preachers are as much a part of the culture as sweet tea and crawdads. Still, Southerners are as prone to leaving Jesus on the sidelines as any group of people. Plenty "sow their wild oats," some for years on end. But when the consequences of their choices finally overwhelm them, they often know better what they need to do. They need to come to Jesus. That's exactly what this Southern prodigal had done. He'd repented and returned.

But in the hours he spent with us, the man expressed a desperation that came out like this: "I've finally found what I need, what we all need, and I have no way to tell my family about it." Those are the words that have replayed in my ears dozens of times in the ensuing years. Because his husbanding and fathering and brothering had been marked by shameful living, the man had estranged himself from nearly everyone he was supposed to have loved. They wanted little or nothing to do with him—even if he was ready to tell them "the greatest story ever told" and how it had changed his life.

As the years have progressed, Jeffrey and I have been put in a position to work with people whose lives echo the experience of this man I met in the Carolina mountains. After years of thinking they could figure life out on their own terms, they had come to recognize the bankruptcy in their God-dismissing pursuits. Their entire life was renewed when they abandoned the kingdoms of their own making for the kingdom of God, accessed by faith in his Son, Jesus Christ. Their hearts knew a joy they had never known before.

Yet the joy was tempered by this great weight: they had not led their children down a path of grace and truth and wonder. Now adults, these children had fulfilled the horrifying words of Harry Chapin's "Cat's in the Cradle." They had mimicked their parents in the pursuit of lesser things. They had no interest in God.

What are these parents to do? Their hearts have been repaired as they have begun their growth in Jesus. The love they rarely demonstrated in any noticeable way when their children were young is the love they want their children to see now. It is the kind of love God inspires: unconditional, generous, instructive, respectful, and empowering. But even more, it is the love that points to Jesus himself, so that others may be led to the faith that ignites God's saving response. These parents want so much for their children to have what they have: a Spirit-woven life that leads to those famous attributes of Galatians 5:22-23 – love, joy, peace, patience, kindness, goodness, faithfulness, gentleness, and self-control. Oh, what a family they could have then!

But the difficulty is always the same. Their children are no longer children. They think and act for themselves. And commonly, their thoughts and actions are governed by their responses to the parents they knew back when they were children. These parents may have demonstrated distance and anger and permissiveness and materialism and conditional acceptance and unrealistic expectations. There is so much pain to go around. The children are hurting, the parents are hurting, the relationships are hurting.

It is inaccurate to suggest, however, that troubled parent-adult child relationships arise only out of sin-ridden parenting. Plenty of parents grew up in homes where mutual respect and grace were prevalent and where God was praised. When it came time for them to do their own parenting, they passed on these family dynamics to their own children. Generations of faithfulness.

But Jesus told a parable that haunts anyone who reads it

soberly. In it, a sower spread seed in anticipation of a harvest. Indeed, many of those seeds did flourish and produce a bumper crop. But others failed. In explaining the parable, Jesus likened the seeds to people who encountered the Good News of the kingdom of God. While some of these people grew tremendously in their faith, many others did not. These "seeds" never really understood the message, or could not last when the heat came, or became choked out by the worries and attractions of life. The Parable of the Sower places no blame on the sower; he did his work faithfully.

In the same way, many parents have maintained their homes with traits opposite to those we saw above. They forged close connections with their children, demonstrated patience, set reasonable and clear boundaries, cultivated their children's individual interests, and were judicious in their expectations. And their children walked away from all that to pursue another course in life. They have become like those dying seeds, and their parents are deeply saddened by what they see in their children's lives today—chiefly, a lack of spiritual interest despite the beauty of Jesus that they were shown when they were little.

Examples like these are never singular points on a map. Rather, they are representations on a spectrum of life. Along this spectrum you will also find those parents who realize now that they were only "playing at religion" when their children were young, those parents who raised their children with signs of real love but without any hint of Jesus, those parents who were presenting Jesus in word but were legalistic or loveless with their children. The variances are perhaps infinite. But what these parents have in common is the pain they now feel over one simple fact: their children are not walking with Jesus.

We want *Love Never Fails* to be a real book. We do not want to dismiss your pain or the possibility that your child will go on living a life outside of God's kingdom. But we intend for this to be a book of hope as well. Prophetic hope, according to the promises of God's word. Prayerful hope, according to the nature of God's grace. And practical hope, with insight into how you might best approach your children with the love of Jesus.

Love Never Fails is not just the title of a book. It is as plain a statement as Scripture makes, found at the outset of 1 Corinthians 13:8. A cynic, even a realist, may ask, "How can this be true? We see the failure of love all around us. People who mean well and care deeply see their love rejected and despised all the time." This is true. But the failure is not in the love; it is in the response. More than that, the kneejerk response that defines failure against the American measure of success is all wrong. The Greek word for "fails" in this passage is *ekpipto*. It means to give out, or to end. Literally, then, true love never fails because it never gives out. Like God's love, it endures through all difficulties. If this is the kind of love you are willing to give in the strength of God's Spirit (the only way in can be given!), then we think this book will be meaningful to you.

When Jesus stood up in the synagogue and chose one passage to read that would point to his purpose on earth, he chose Isaiah 61 and proclaimed, "The Spirit of the Sovereign Lord is upon me." That passage goes on to describe the ministry of the Messiah, the one who would save his people. Included in that ministry are these tremendous words:

"...to comfort all who mourn,
And provide for those who grieve in Zion—

to bestow on them a crown of beauty
  instead of ashes,
the oil of gladness
  instead of mourning,
and a garment of praise
  instead of a spirit of despair."
They will be called oaks of righteousness,
  a planting of the Lᴏʀᴅ
  for the display of his splendor."

If you recognize in this passage both the grief you possess in your spirit for your adult children and the desire you still have for what their life may become, you already share our heart and mind. Let's see where we can go together from here.

Jeff Hopper
April 2012

Right now, God is actively devising a way to restore your child to himself. He is far more grieved by the separation of your child from him than you are. More than that, he is far more capable of doing something about it.

1 TWO SIDES TO EVERY STORY?

F OR ALL ITS WEALTH, the Bible is not really a manual on family relationships. What it does have to say is usually simple—"honor your father and mother"—or reflective—"a wise son brings joy to his father." Rarer are points of instruction for the everyday situations we find ourselves in as parents and children. In a way this is confounding. It would be good to know God's mind on how long to support children who are too dreamy in their aspirations or when it is time to put our aging parents under another's care.

It is confounding to us as authors as well, because we are able to write (and speak) most confidently when the word of God is thorough and plain. We lose the concern we have over our own fallibilities in teaching and interpretation and simply convey the revealed words of the Lord.

But where the Bible is sometimes quiet in word, it is perfectly consistent in pointing us to its author. The same Lord who breathed Scripture into those who first inked the ancient scrolls is the Spirit of God who guides us today. Where his word is silent, his voice is not. In fact, we are most completely and most personally informed when we rely on the Spirit and the word.

In this book, you may find us teaching without specific scriptural support. This is not because we don't want you to know what God has said in his word, but rather because the word does not offer direct insight into how we might handle every situation. In these circumstances, we are left to draw the wisdom of the Lord from the experiences God has given the people of the Bible and the words he spoke into their lives by the Holy Spirit. This makes us, in many ways, no more and no less equipped than God's people of old. They had even less Scripture than we do, relying on the Pentateuch alone, if that (the Pentateuch is the first five books of the Bible, containing the early history of the Hebrew people and the law that God gave them to live by). These people relied on God's prophets—the pronouncing voices of God's revealed mind—and the answers from God that they received to their own inquiries of him.

It is to these ancient people we turn in recognition of the truth behind this chapter's title: that there is more than one side to every story.

A shepherd, a warrior, a poet, a king, David was a man of God. He loved the Lord and loved his law. So it is certain that as he studied the early word of God, he was familiar with this principal passage of faith and family found in the scrolls of the Pentateuch:

> "These commandments that I give you today are to be on your hearts. Impress them on your children. Talk about them when you sit at home and when you walk along the road, when you lie down and when you get up. Tie them as symbols on your hands and bind them on your foreheads.

Write them on the doorframes of your houses and on your gates." (Deuteronomy 6:6-9)

From the beginning of his specific instruction through his law, God intended for the practiced faith of his people to be integrated into all that they did. Moreover, it was meant to belong to all of them—not just adults, not just men, not just the super-religious among them. Faith in God, demonstrated by an understanding of his law and adherence to it, belonged to the whole household: fathers, mothers, children. We might say it even belonged to the doorposts!

Surely David, desiring to identify with the blessed man of Psalm 1 who delighted in the law of the Lord, knew this passage from Deuteronomy. He would have tried to pass on his faith to his children.

But David was also a sinner, a man prone to disobedience even in his wisdom and experience. His passion for God was displaced by his passion for women—and not just Bathsheba, whom he infamously seized from marriage to another man and took for his own, abusing all kingly authority. David accumulated wives for himself, ignoring the due warning of God: "[The king] must not take many wives, or his heart will be led astray" (Deuteronomy 17:17). We cannot know what impact this broadening family had on David's ability to raise and teach his children according to the word of the Lord, but we do know that as David's life progressed and his children grew, he faced one of the most gut-wrenching episodes of his life.

As we read in 2 Samuel, beginning in the thirteenth chapter, trouble arose in David's house of half-brothers and sisters when his son Amnon "fell in love" with David's daughter Tamar. Devising a plan to ensnare Tamar, Amnon seized her when they were alone. Although she resisted in the name of

Israel, Amnon overpowered and raped his sister. She went away in disgrace when Amnon refused to have anything more to do with her, "hating her more than he had loved her."

Tamar's full brother Absalom came to her aid. He took Tamar into his home and bided his time for revenge. When two years had passed, Absalom arranged to trap Amnon outside the view of their father. At a party thrown by Absalom, Amnon became drunk and unaware. Absalom ordered his men to strike Amnon dead and they complied.

> **Tracking the Story**
>
> **Read the full account in 2 Samuel, chapters 13-15**
>
> David: King of Judah and head of the household
>
> Absalom: David's son
>
> Tamar: Absalom's sister
>
> Amnon: half-brother of Absalom and Tamar

Absalom fled and David received news of the murder. The king fell into despair over the loss of Amnon, grieving openly with his other sons and his servants. Three years passed, with Absalom living in self-imposed exile, and in this time the king was consoled. In his heart, he longed to see Absalom and restore their broken relationship. But hearts are not always strong enough to provoke action in us. David had to be charged twice over by the commander of his army, Joab—first to return Absalom to Jerusalem and then, after two more years had passed, to bring his son into his courts. When the two were finally reunited, David kissed his son, the closing words of 2 Samuel 14.

Absalom, the Scripture tells us, was a handsome man with enviably thick hair. That is, he was in appearance someone his father could have taken pride in. But Absalom's actions led to increasing pain for David. His father had seen rape and murder in his house; soon he would see treachery.

The opening verses of 2 Samuel 15 tell us that "in the

course of time" Absalom conspired against the rule of his father. By charisma and craft, he gathered men to him, men who would not hesitate to rebel against the old men and their old ways. Finally, a messenger came to David with this conclusive report: "The hearts of the men of Israel are with Absalom." David's authority was gone. So that lives could be saved and plans could be made, David ordered the evacuation of the palace. In his leaving, David went so far as to refer to his son as "King Absalom."

The days that followed were laced with horror. David was openly cursed as he passed through the countryside. Absalom lay in full public view with the concubines David had left to tend the palace. A once trusted counselor of David who had turned coat to Absalom's side hanged himself when he found that his counsel was now disdained by both men. Finally, Absalom was speared through by Joab, despite David's command that his son be gently treated should he be captured.

The household of David, though restored to the palace and the throne, was overwhelmed. The king himself wept violently at the news of his son's death—an act that spited the work of the men who had protected him and turned their victory into mourning.

All in all, the story of David and Absalom carries too much melodrama for even our modern scriptwriters, whose works play on a hundred cable channels. But in its complexity we see a mirror on the stories of our own families. There is David's side of the story, with a father and king utterly disrespected by his son. There is Absalom's side of the story, with a son too harshly treated for avenging an unrighteous act. And there are the sides of so many others—Joab, the mothers, the counselors, the concubines—all caught in the churning wake of a family gone awry.

To ask whether this picture of a torn family hits home is to invoke a double entendre. If you are reading this book, it is because you recognize a rift in your family. Particularly between you and your adult children. Particularly over the matter of faith in Jesus. And as much as you would like to think that you are without blame in the matter (or maybe that you are to blame and that your child is completely innocent), the nearly universal truth is that trouble comes from every quarter. You are culpable; so is your child.

But there is good news. Where we are guilty, we are forgivable. God makes a way for restoration.

In 2 Samuel 14, right in the midst of the David and Absalom accounts, we find this stunning promise, delivered by a woman sent to provoke reconciliatory action from David: "God does not take away life; instead, he devises ways so that a banished person may not remain estranged from him." No doubt you are reading this book because you are deeply troubled by what you see in your adult children. They are estranged from God. And as it stands now, your perspective on their life's choices is that the chance for a recovered relationship is almost certainly zero. May we encourage you in this moment? Right now, God is actively devising a way to restore your child to himself. He is far more grieved by the separation of your child from him than you are. More than that, he is far more capable of doing something about it. "God," you have assuredly heard it said, "is on your side." He is. But in addition to that, he is on the side of your child—no matter how dreadful your family story has been in the past or is right now. You see, there are in truth three sides to your family story: yours, your child's and God's.

Letting God be God
In the weeks leading up to the completion of this book, we

were reminded in numerous conversations with adult parents and each other just how difficult it can be to let God take over the story. Many of the parents we regularly work with have achieved levels of worldly success, particularly in matters of business and finance. Among them are entrepreneurs, investors, and executives who may look back on their careers and see the positive results of the business decisions they have made. Even those friends who have not "made big money," so to speak, generally live rewarded American lives, where their careful planning and conservative choices have resulted in some of the pleasures of success: a comfortable home, relaxing vacations, education for their children. When a couple can look back on a personal history like this, they have much to thank God for. But because of our human tendencies, what we often do instead is look back with greater and greater self-confidence. We think, *If I succeeded before, certainly the decisions I make next will succeed as well.* And we make the stunning error of forgetting God's preeminent role in all we have and do.

The ancient kings of Israel and Judah were notorious for this kind of behavior. God would provide them with victories in battle, bringing protection for their people and material resources into their kingdoms. Yet over and over, the kings would turn to their own "best wisdom" or manipulative practices, and all God's good would be reversed.

King Saul, the first in the line of the ancient Hebrew kings, established this eventually well-worn thread of self-guided manipulative leadership. A review of his actions provides us an important contrast between the type of leadership we may be used to practicing and the type of leadership God intends for us.

In 1 Samuel 15, Saul came to a place of battle, defeating the Amalekites, capturing their king, and seizing their best livestock. Sounds like a victory! However, God had specifically directed Saul to spare nothing; he wanted the Amalekites completely destroyed. Saul thought better of it. Capturing the Amalekite king gave him a "trophy" for boasting, and keeping the best animals just seemed like common sense. But as we have nearly all read in Isaiah 55:19 ("'For my thoughts are not your thoughts, neither are your ways my ways,' declares the LORD"), common sense is not always God's sense. The Lord has designs that defy our best reasoning. When we ignore this supreme principle of God's universe, we can find ourselves grappling with the consequences of our self-governance. Saul's actions sent the final message to God that he had no real interest in the ways of the Lord. Because of this, God sent the prophet Samuel to the king—and the words he delivered land us right in the midst of our present lesson. Samuel reminded Saul, "Although you were once small in your own eyes, did you not become the head of the tribes of Israel? The LORD anointed you king over Israel." The whole of Saul's success came from God. But when it came time to add to that success, Saul chose his own course of action, rather than the one God had given him. For this, God brought Saul a new "reward": he rejected Saul as king over Israel.

Saul attempted contrition, but it was too late for the king, and as we discover in the ensuing accounts of Saul's leader-

> **Tracking the Story**
>
> **Read the full account in 1 Samuel, chapter 15**
>
> Saul: First king of Judah
>
> Amalekites: the people Saul was told to defeat and completely destroy
>
> Samuel: God's principal prophet in Judah during Saul's reign
>
> David: God's anointed successor to Saul
>
> Jonathan: Saul's son and David's dearest friend

ship, he was not really contrite at all. Indeed, he turned his manipulative designs against God's new choice for king, David. After the young shepherd's victory over Goliath and in spite of David's friendship with Saul's son Jonathan, we see the lame duck king contrive a murderous plan for David at the New Moon festival in 1 Samuel 20. When David slipped out of town thanks to Jonathan's warning, Saul's heart was revealed in his rage, and he hurled his spear at his own son.

Bent on David's demise, Saul pursued his anointed successor with increasing intent, even killing the entire household of God's priests at Nod because they had assisted David. To the end, Saul's life deteriorated, included a visit to the witch at Endor, who herself rebuked Saul for turning to her God-despised counsel.

In contrast, David had multiple opportunities to take Saul's life. He refused, for the singular reason that God had not ordained this role for him. He knew the king's death would come in God's time; there was no chance he would act outside of God's leading. Yes, David too would go forward in life to make mistakes of his own. But he never despised the Lord's instruction or fashioned a way around it. He wanted to know what God wanted of him, and most often he followed this path.

It should be no surprise to us, then, that the line leading to Jesus came down not through Saul, but through David. In John 5, when Jesus was challenged about the things he was doing (including healing people on the Sabbath), he responded by explaining that his actions were not birthed through his own initiative. Listen:

> "Very truly I tell you, the Son can do nothing by himself; he can do only what he sees his Father doing, because whatever the Father does the Son also does... By myself I

> can do nothing; I judge only as I hear, and my judgment is
> just, for I seek not to please myself but him who sent me."
> (John 5:19, 30)

Jesus clearly made room for the Father's leading in his life. He would never have dreamed of implementing his own design!

What does all this mean for parents of adult children? Why are we taking this somewhat circuitous route through Scripture? Two reasons: When we relate to our children—and even more so our adult children—we need to keep reminding ourselves that God is Lord over all aspects of our lives. And we find in David and Jesus the example of this kind of living.

When instead we attempt to orchestrate circumstances in the same way we have done elsewhere in our lives, thinking this will bring us certain success, we are actually imposing our will on God. We expect of him things he may not have in his plans. That's dangerous ground to tread! True spiritual authority rests with God alone. When we try to exercise authority outside of his boundaries, no matter how moral or "right" we think we are in our actions, we have usurped God's place in our lives. We have turned instead to a counterfeit authority, standing on our position as "the parents" or our history of earthly success by self-management. When we go that way, we part from Jesus, who used his highest spiritual authority to lay down his life. More than this, Jesus called us to do the same: "If anyone would come after me, he must deny himself and take up his cross daily and follow me" (Luke 9:23, NIV 1984). As foreign as this may sound to our proactive 21st Century ears, God wants to take charge of our lives. He wants us to set aside the ways of the world to follow him.

Admittedly, this kind of surrender can be confusing. We would not be surprised to hear you ask, "Am I supposed to sit back and do nothing?" Not exactly. But you are certainly not supposed to do the work that belongs to God alone. Surely you would not, for instance, suggest that it is your job to save your children. And yet many parents do all they can to ordain the circumstances that they think will lead to their child's salvation. Understand: God's plans contain every last detail. When we stick our foot or nose in where it does not belong, we are staking a claim to his supremacy. But there is good news in recognizing all this as well, for if we give God his rightful position as the Lord of our family relationships, tremendous self-imposed pressure is lifted from our shoulders. When we cast off from our descriptions of ourselves titles like "judge," "authority," or "head," we are able to begin attaining the role God really has for us, which is: Holy-Spirit infused servant of the Lord. We don't do the work for God. We come alongside him in the work he is already doing. When we function in this mode, we will honor God in whatever place of authority he lends to us. As parents, this frees us to love without ulterior motives and covert operations.

Finally, when we allow God his ultimate place in our lives and the lives of our children, we begin to see what God is really up to: developing *us*. If we truly take the time to learn the ways of God's kingdom—as opposed to simply transferring our well-practiced worldly methods to our Christian life—our walk with Jesus will be deepened beyond imagination. Could it be that God intends for your frustrations and concerns about your adult children to be the training ground for your own relationship with him? Of course!

As you continue to read through this relatively short book, you will find that we offer some practical suggestions for establishing God-centered, grace-filled friendships with your children. But none of these instructions is more valuable than the simple truth we hope you have discovered in these last few pages—that God's way is far better than any method or trick we can devise. In fact, if we push our way around like a bully on God's playground, what we may eventually see in our children is either sterner resistance or a grudging acceptance (that is, a joyless salvation—which is hardly the life God has in mind for any of us!). So our best instruction is this, and you'll find it again and again: Talk to God. Listen to him. As Jesus said, he is not only the truth and the life; he is the way. And his way brings freedom, both for us and our children. So let the way before you be his alone.

We must recognize that when we attempt to parent our adult children as if our own strength or wisdom or determination will do the trick of returning them to God, we are acting faithlessly. It is God's kindness and the Spirit's conviction that lead any man or woman to repentance.

2 ANGUISH MET

M OST PEOPLE READ only the good parts of the Bible. You may be one of these, happy to find the blessings and not so sure about the rest. The irony there is that even the blessings can be troubling. "Blessed," Jesus said, "are those who mourn." Yes, he was pointing to the comfort they would receive, but look at what must come first. Mourning. Grief. Anguish.

It is hard to be a parent for an excellent reason: love. While we may be deeply moved by reports of a distant catastrophe and the thousands of children lost there, and while we may identify with the circumstances in the lives of others who tell us their stories of pain, nothing hurts like love. When our own child chooses a course that we know can lead to big trouble—particularly activities that do not honor the instructions of God regarding temperance, sexuality, materialism, and relationships—it is hard to stand back and watch, even though we know they are not children under our thumb anymore. While they may not recognize the external effect of their actions, we are feeling it deeply, and it pains us. Though God says we should not, we worry. Though our doctor says we should not, we worry. And we do so out of love.

In the course of just a few sentences, we have actually opened up several lines of thought, and we want to take some time now to address these one by one over the course of this chapter and those that follow. They are:

- The actions of our children
- The age of our children
- The definition of love
- The application of our love

The actions of our children

All actions carry weight. In the beginning, when Adam and Eve walked in the garden with God, he laid out for them a single instruction: do not eat the fruit you find on the tree of the knowledge of good and evil. Every other tree was fine. This one tree was not.

Now consider this carefully, because we all know what happened: Adam and Eve disobeyed God. They ate the fruit of the one forbidden tree. But why?

The fruit, we know, was attractive. It had sensory appeal. If the fruit had been prickly all around like a pineapple, or smelled like the infamous durian, or hung high in the tree like dates, Adam and Eve may have walked away from the temptation offered to them by the enemy, Satan.

Adam and Eve's resistance was also met with a crafty explanation by Satan. He told them that they would become like God in their discernment of all things if only they ate of this fruit. In other words, they chose to believe that their sin would *improve* them. How could this be bad?

But perhaps the reason Adam and Eve went ahead with their action was this: they did not think it would affect anyone but themselves. Some choices in life are obviously self-serving. Other actions have an undeniable ill effect on others—perhaps intentionally so. But here was a sin—eating a fruit—that did not appear up-front to possess any possible consequences. In fact, the only apparent difficulty with eating the fruit was that God had directed them not to. Surely he had made some sort of mistake, however, for this action would bring them closer to him in understanding.

So Adam and Eve reasoned away their disobedience. They did what looked and felt really good to them. And God fell by the wayside.

This, friends, is the definition of sin in a nutshell: we depart from God. And we cannot emphasize with enough vigor how important it is to keep this in mind when we relate to our children and react to the sin in their own life—for we were the generation before them, and our own sin always precedes theirs!

When our children are small, we are, frankly, their "God." That is, we are the ones delivering direct, unexplained instructions like "don't throw your food on the floor," "time to go to bed and go to sleep," and "keep your seatbelt on." We might try explaining to a two-year-old the good reasons behind these dictates, but we accomplish greater success through negative reinforcement, usually involving physical restraint or minor infliction of pain.

It doesn't take long, however, for our children to reach the stage of *why*. They want to know the reasons behind the directions you are giving and the boundaries you are establishing. So you explain. Food on the floor makes an extra chore for Mommy. Not getting your rest makes you a less happy person and can lead to illness. Taking off your seatbelt brings the risk of violent injury in an accident. You may be a patient fielder of all these inquiries and you may give outstanding reasons behind your rules. And yet your children will still disobey, testing the limits of your leadership and the severity of your discipline.

As your children grow older, you will move toward nuanced instruction. Yes, you want your children to respect their elders and speak up when meeting new people… but you also want them to be cautious around strangers and learn to protect themselves against predators. You teach your children to assess their environment and recognize when it may be okay to deviate from an otherwise absolute instruction. Additionally, if you are a Christian parent, you will begin to shed your own absolute authority and point your children toward the real source of many of your instructions: God. For instance, you may have candid conversations with your maturing children about sexuality, and while some of what you say may have to do with the practical matters of emotional readiness or STDs, you emphasize God's greater standards of purity of mind, heart, and body. Your children may respond favorably to your conversations, and yet they will still seek answers on their own, sometimes in conversations with others they respect but also through sinful "sowing of their oats."

Do you see the pattern here? Children sin. Children keep sinning. In this way they are entirely like their parents. And the older our children become, the more like us they may be— for their ability to reason and act independently leads them to experiment beyond our reach. When this is done apart from God's will for them, we grieve as God does. Our children's sin has an effect beyond themselves, even when they think that (a) they are acting on their own and (b) we should not really care. How we respond to this sin is important, especially as our children move out from under our provision, and we will examine this difference according to age shortly. Before we move on, however, we must recognize a definition of sin that applies to us perhaps more notably than it does to our children. We find it in Paul's letter to the Romans.

...everything that does not come from faith is sin. (Romans 14:23b)

We are very good at compiling a checklist of rights and wrongs we call sin. And indeed, God would call many of these things sin as well. But if you need a more broad-brushed measure, here it is. *The absence of faith is the presence of sin.* When our children push aside the ways of God and act in their own "wisdom," they have forsaken faith in God and his word. They have assumed that they can rightly judge what is best for their life, apart from God's instruction. They have, shall we say, pulled an Adam and Eve. But with eyes to ourselves, we must in honesty recognize that when we attempt to parent our adult children as if our own strength or wisdom or determination will do the trick of returning them to God, we too are acting faithlessly. It is God's kindness and the Spirit's conviction that leads any man or woman to repentance. When we make an effort to act over and above this truth—rather than alongside it in humility and prayer—then we are in essence usurping God's role. Can we demonstrate less faith? No. We never want to meet sin with sin. Instead, we want to throw our lives and our children's lives into God's arms. We want to—in faith—depend on him for all things, including the rescue of our children from their departure from God.

The age of our children

As you may have noticed in our progression of a child's development several paragraphs back, we stopped short of the stage of life this book is written to address: adult children. While it is common to think of parenting as "done" when a child turns 18 or moves out from under our provision, the span of "adult childhood" is far longer, and the love of a parent does not simply die during this time.

When I (JH) was pastoring a church several years ago, I sat in conversation with one of the men of our church who was struggling through the costly decisions of one of his children. He said to me, "You're children are so good." That could mean a thousand things, of course, but what he meant was that my three sons—two of whom were in high school at the time—did not seem to be making choices damaging to their walk of faith. My response was cautious: "My boys haven't been to college yet." We all recognize the average college scene to be fraught with temptations of every kind, activities the Bible summarizes in a word: debauchery. Far too many "good kids" shipwreck their Christian commitment on the rocks of college campus looseness. And far too many parents find themselves grieving over the suddenly godless decisions of their apparently well-raised children.

But this is only the beginning of adulthood. We have found ourselves across the table from much older parents, lamenting the choices of their much older children. We are speaking of children in their forties and fifties who have been entangled in alcoholism, drug addiction, domestic violence, job loss, divorce—all causing deep separations between themselves and God and deep anguish in their parents.

Life endures. And with it, sometimes troubles never seem to go away. There are times and situations when older parents must separate themselves from their wayward children. The literal and figurative jails that lock in children who have crossed every reasonable line serve a purpose that sometimes a parent so close to his or her child cannot. But even in the grip of these soul-crushing times, love remains. A parent with means uses it to rescue a child: money spent for attorneys and counselors and rehabilitations—not to get the child "off" but to buy another chance to finally break their children free of the sins and consequences that have ruled their lives. Others without so much money use whatever resources they can—social networks and social programs—to find a way out for their beloved child.

There is an ebb and flow to all this activity. When a parent rescues an adult child and that child yet returns to the gutter of their ill choices, it is matter of course for many parents to say, "I'm done with him. I've done all I can do and he's still an ungrateful, undeserving fool." A season of estrangement (more a sabbatical than a separation) ensues; the parent simply needs to rest and regroup from the emotional nature of the circumstances. In time, however, the parent softens in heart and begins to look for a new avenue of assistance. The thought of love remains, *How can I help my child?*

It is important to turn to Scripture here and see the biblical undergirding for both the ebb and flow of love and the relentless pursuit of a child's best life.

A recurring Old Testament description of God goes like this:

"You are a forgiving God, gracious and compassionate, slow to anger and abounding in love."

Though taken here from Nehemiah 9:17, a description very similar to this is found also in Exodus, Numbers, Psalms, Joel and Jonah. God—in his own words, or the words of his prophets and kings—is forgiving, gracious, compassionate, slow to anger, and abounding in love. Can we find any better definition of what a parent should be?

Yet we know this. Though slow in his anger, God's patience with his children, the people of Israel, did run out. And by exile in Assyria, Babylon, Egypt, and distant lands, God established a season of separation between himself and his people.

Through the prophet Hosea, God announced that his people's waywardness was like the infidelity of a wife turned harlot—not a pretty picture. When his patience for this behavior had run out, God pronounced a season of judgment on his people.

> "She has not acknowledged that I was the one
>   who gave her the grain, the new wine and oil,
> who lavished on her the silver and gold—
>   which they used for Baal.
> Therefore I will take away my grain when it ripens,
>   and my new wine when it is ready.
> I will take back my wool and my linen,
>   intended to cover her naked body.
> So now I will expose her lewdness
>   before the eyes of her lovers...
> I will stop all her celebrations:
>   her yearly festivals, her New Moons,
>   her Sabbath days—all her appointed festivals.
> I will ruin her vines and her fig trees,
>   which she said were her pay from her lovers;
> I will make them a thicket,
>   and wild animals will devour them.
> I will punish her for the days
>   she burned incense to the Baals;
> she decked herself with rings and jewelry,
>   and went after her lovers,
>   but me she forgot,"
>   declares the Lord. (Hosea 2:8-13)

This is a parent whose joy in his children had ceased. He was cutting off all expressions of graciousness and love. But you will notice where we have removed one line from these prophetic words by way of an ellipsis (...). Look at that line now:

"...no one will take her out of my hands."

God—though a parent still loving and caring for and guarding his child—released her to "the wilds" for time enough to allow her to understand the gravity of her sin, precisely as it effected the relationship between him (the Father) and her (the child). And all the while God maintained the hope of restoration:

"Therefore I am now going to allure her;
   I will lead her into the wilderness
   and speak tenderly to her.
There I will give her back her vineyards,
   and will make the Valley of Achor a door of hope.
There she will respond as in the days of her youth,
   as in the day she came up out of Egypt." (Hosea 2:14-15)

It is crucial to understand that Achor means "trouble." It was in the Valley of Trouble—trouble of his children's own making—that God intended to gain his people's attention and draw them back to him. God will not yank his children out of the trouble before it has served its purpose, which is to awaken their ears to his ever-calling voice of love, a love that always and forever abounds.

Here we are led to consider the difference between children still under our provision and those who have moved out. It is more appropriate for us to step in to the choices and circumstances of our smaller children, our teenage children, and even our collegiate children. Their decisions have a practical bearing on the operation of our home. So we are more hands-on in confronting their bad behavior and disciplining for change. We are also quicker to step in and discourage, prevent and rescue our child from damaging activities. But both of these approaches transition over time. As our children grow older, we allow the consequences of their actions to apply their weight to our children, knowing that these consequences may be our children's best teacher in the years to come.

The role of the parent of an adult child is to care, as we would for a beloved friend who has also overstepped the boundaries of temperance or propriety.

It is not our role to micromanage, intervening at each and every step. It is not our role to lecture or preach to our adult children, especially when they do not have ears to hear. It is not our role to chastise our adult children, or to beg righteousness from them for our sake, or to shame them in order "to whip them into shape."

It is our role, as parents who desire to honor and reflect our Lord in all things, to do just that. We are meant, as in all things, to bring glory to God in the way that we parent our adult children. Therefore, it is our role to remain steadfast in our love for our children, no matter their decisions and actions. And it is to that very role that we turn our attention in the chapter ahead.

We might find it far easier to teach Sunday school to sixth graders than to be patient with an adult son who won't commit to a career or hold our anger in check with an adult daughter who has come for another loan when the last one was frittered away.

3 LOVE DEFINED

WHEN YOU STOOD in front of the altar on the day of your wedding, there is a high probability that the officiant took a few moments to read the heart of the thirteenth chapter of Paul's first letter to the Corinthians. And there is an even greater probability that you didn't hear a word that minister was saying! Such is the state of mind of a man or woman occupied with romance on the most important day of their lives...

Hopefully, you have had the opportunity to return to that remarkable chapter in the years since your wedding. In fact, we find it interesting that for all the emphasis placed on the so-called spiritual disciplines of Scripture reading and fasting, meditation and prayer, so little focus has been given to the practical living out of love as it is presented to us in 1 Corinthians 13.

In this chapter, we intend to dig deeply into this remarkable list. We may say that we love our spouse or our children, but if we rarely dare to view that love through the lens of God's definition of the greatest characteristic a person can possess, then we can find ourselves in the locale of that proverbial misguided ship: a half a degree off at the beginning and hundreds of miles from landfall in the end. So walk with us through a review of this passage, which we present here in full, then review piece by piece.

> Love is patient, love is kind. It does not envy, it does not boast, it is not proud. It does not dishonor others, it is not self-seeking, it is not easily angered, it keeps no record of wrongs. Love does not delight in evil but rejoices with the truth. It always protects, always trusts, always hopes, always perseveres.
>
> Love never fails. (1 Corinthians 13:4-8a)

In the broad sweep of the context, we recognize in only a moment that we are presented with a very demanding list. Indeed, if you find it hard to make room for daily Bible study, try keeping your demeanor kind, your heart humble, or your actions selfless at all times! We might find it far easier to teach Sunday school to sixth graders, take our turn in the prayer chain, or even join the door-to-door evangelism team than to be patient with an adult son who won't commit to a career or hold our anger in check with an adult daughter who has come for another loan when the last one was frittered away.

As an ideal, perhaps love never does fail. But as a practice left to the best efforts of the average parent, it fails all the time. No wonder we hesitate to go back, open this passage and hold ourselves to it. And yet, that is what we will try to do now.

Yes, it is our children who can cause us to suffer longest.

Love is patient

You might recognize almost instantly the connection between this opening identifier of love and the Old Testament passages that describe God who, we were told, is "slow to anger." Paul begins by drawing a parallel between who God is and who we should be—an admonition in perfect keeping with his instruction just two chapters earlier: "Follow my example, as I follow the example of Christ" (1 Corinthians 11:1). Our cues must come from the Lord.

The Greek (*makrothymeō*) for demonstrating patience hits hard; it means to "suffer long." Few parents need to be told that, when taken literally, this is the common trajectory of their role! Even when we willingly welcome children into the midst of our marriages and comfortable routines, they demand far more of us than we reasonably expect. They test our patience in the short-term, screaming for small reasons at the most inconvenient times. And they test our patience in the long-term, returning to the same errors we have discussed with them over and over. And now that they are adults, where they should be moving from being our charges to our caregivers, they still make faulty decisions of significant consequence. They do not *know better*, as we were certain they would by now. Yes, it is our children who can cause us to suffer longest.

If change is what we really want to see in our children's hearts, shouldn't we pattern our interaction with them after the coaxing method God himself uses?

Love is kind

Paul completes an obvious pairing to begin this definition of love that God inspired in him. When we lose patience, we frequently lose kindness as well. We speak with exasperation—which comes quite naturally to one who is exasperated! And when our words turn rash, they reveal ugliness over beauty. In that moment, no one would call us kind.

We are required to note initially then that the presentation of love as God would have it is not quick on the trigger. It holds back when it is most tempted to leap forward and make a point. It recognizes that while actions may change (temporarily) under the burden of another's red-faced bluster, hearts rarely do. When I (JH) was called upon to arbitrate an escalated encounter between my sons in their childhood days, I often found myself explaining to my boys that the response to an ill action, if it is loud or violent, is often far worse than the original action itself. The "harmed one" may cloud my view of the "harmer" if the tables are turned too belligerently. The same is true in our confrontation of others, including our adult children. Their words or actions may deserve an unfavorable response. But when that response comes with roughshod fierceness, the one who first acted wrongly may go away saying, "I thought *I* was bad…" The chance for healing and a heart change may well escape with our judgmental, overpowering, unloving response. We are told in Romans 2:4 that it is God's kindness that leads to repentance. If change is what we really want to see in our children's hearts, shouldn't we pattern our interaction with them after the coaxing method God himself uses?

You may be asking two questions at this point. First, you may ask how this is at all possible. You must recognize both patience and kindness as part of the fruit that the Holy Spirit produces in us (Galatians 5:22-23). Certainly, without the Holy Spirit's empowering, we cannot love like God. There is no other way to do as he does.

Second, you may be asking if there is to be no end to our patience. Shall we never speak up? By the Father's example in the Old Testament, by the Son's example in the New Testament, and by Paul's instructions regarding those who would not be otherwise moved, there is an ultimate time for action. God sent the Israelites into exile, Jesus stuck his foot in the Pharisees' door and sternly addressed their many faulty practices, and Paul wrote to these same Corinthians that an immoral man should be handed "over to Satan, so that the sinful nature may be destroyed and his spirit saved on the day of the Lord" (1 Corinthians 5:5). Patience does not mean ongoing inaction. It acts with purpose and sometimes with severity, but it does so with dignity maintained for both the giver and the receiver, and with the enduring hope that Christ will be believed and redemption made for the one who is far from him now.

When the Spirit moves through us and we render the fruit he is developing in us, we accomplish everything that really matters to God.

Love does not envy

Because, in the common vernacular, envy is frequently confused with covetousness—to desire what another possesses— you might be surprised to find that the Greek foundation of the word (*zēlóō*) points to zeal and may be applied positively. It is with righteous jealousy that God desires our worship and obedience; he wishes us never to surrender these pursuits to another affection, to an idol. We too may zealously seek Christ, "envying" his presence and his nature.

But zeal, like fire, can burn in warmth or in destruction. The religious leaders of Jesus' day were certainly zealous for adherence to the law. And in their zeal, they believed that everyone else should be just like them. The trouble was that they lacked love. They disdained those who did not live up to their external standards. Sadly, we may find that our parenting tends in the same direction. We hold fast to secondary issues but present them as essential, letting those around us—and especially those close to us, like our children—know that they aren't in our good graces if they don't live life as we do. Don't get us wrong here. There are absolutes that God requires of us, but when we hold to these as if they permit us to be impersonal and unresponsive to the ideas and feelings of others, we miss "the more important matters of the law" (Matthew 23:23). Going back to the fruit of the Spirit, we find an amazing statement at the end of the list: "Against such things there is no law" (Galatians 5:24). What are those things? Love, joy, peace, patience, kindness, goodness, faithfulness, gentleness, and self-control. Stunning. No theological constructs here, nothing that looks like doctrine. And yet when the Spirit moves through us and we render the fruit he is developing in us, we accomplish everything that really matters to God. We don't have to present ourselves as zealots for a cause when we begin with zeal for the Spirit's active, present work in us.

Before we move on, let's acknowledge that the Greek *zēlóō* can mean plainly "don't envy" in the way that we would readily understand it. On the surface, we may be slow to recognize how this would apply to our interaction with our children. Surely the problem is not that we envy what they have. Not so fast! We all speak glowingly of the free spiritedness that young children possess, of the way they live without the weight of responsibility. With the perspective of age, we know we should not pine for this extensive free spiritedness in our own lives—we would just look silly! But as we and our children grow older, their youthful traits may actually become an unhealthy attraction to us. We'd like some of their laid back nature and the leisure time that accompanies it. And when we can't get it, frustration is born out of envy. We find ourselves saying things like: "Our generation is working, saving, providing—this can't be said for the younger generation." Indeed, many a mid-life crisis leaps from our envy of our adult children, with their idealism and energy. But so much of this is grasping for former things. It signifies a desire to return to the work God did in us *then*, as opposed to the work he is doing in us *now*. You see, such envy stands against maturing love. If we recognize it in ourselves, we must turn from it—zealously!

God loved us when we were completely unlovable in terms of the things we had accomplished. We had failed both to do the things God wanted us to do and to avoid the things he didn't want us to do. And yet he loved us.

Love does not boast

Like burgers sold at McDonald's, we would be the bazillionth people to write about generation gaps if we set off on that course here. We'll limit it to this one observation: generation gaps have much to do with the presumed superiority of one generation over another. The old know they are wise—and let those who are younger know it by their unsolicited advice and sermonettes. The young know they are progressive—and let those who are older know it by the unveiled exasperation of shaking heads or the intentional insertion of provocative ideas and phrases.

It's all a game that says, "We know better than you."

And it has nothing to do with love.

Love, Paul wrote to the Corinthians, does not seek to establish oneself as better than another. In families, specifically, significant pain emerges from conflicts where one person suggests his or her superiority. But this is something that parents must be most careful to guard against. In a way, they have "been there before." They have made the mistakes and learned the lessons and found success. From that, they have been an agent of provision for their children, commonly giving them not only the necessities of life but plenty of extras as well. And parents presume that all this figuring out that they have done places them in a lasting position of authority over their children, even when their children have gone forward and done well for themselves. "You know, I'd done that by the time I was 25," may sound like a simple bit of storytelling to a parent. But to an adult child, it can represent a criticism, if not a boastful challenge that sounds just like this: "So when are you going to get *your* act together?"

True love recognizes that its source comes from the God who first loved us. And he did this, we read in Romans 5:6-8, at a time "when we were still powerless...while we were still sinners." Simply, God loved us when we were completely unlovable in terms of the things we had accomplished. We had failed both to do the things God wanted us to do and to avoid the things he didn't want us to do. And yet he loved us.

The gospel turns this idea even more upside-down from the way we would approach things. For Jesus did not come and pronounce his superiority as the one who would save us by his death. Instead, he came and took "the very nature of a servant...he humbled himself and became obedient to death—even death on a cross!" (Philippians 2:7-8). Suddenly, it all becomes so clear. Jesus loved in humility, the opposite of which is boasting. It is not our job to tell our children how much better we are than they are—how much more we have experienced, how much more we have learned, how much more we have achieved. It is our job to convey to our children by our words and our actions that we are doing our very best to attempt to live *under* the rule of the Lord, who is Jesus. If we can accomplish this so that Jesus truly shines through us, his vessels, we will make advances in our relationships with our children that we could never make by telling them how good we are and how much we have to offer them.

Our error as earthly parents is that we often launch our boasting from the pad of our children's earthly successes... But none compares to the deepening spiritual growth we want our children to experience.

Love is not proud

While much of what we have written about love not being boastful could be repeated here, allow us to take a different view when we consider that love is not proud.

It is within the nature of parents—and we believe the boundaries of Scripture—for parents to take a measure of pride in the successes of their children, particularly if these are spiritual strengths. Consider that Paul said of the Corinthians, "I know your eagerness to help, and I have been boasting about it to the Macedonians," and of the Thessalonians, "among God's churches, we boast about your perseverance and faith." These were Paul's spiritual children. If they were showing Christ in the way they were serving one another, Paul told others.

Our error as earthly parents, however, is that we often launch our boasting from the pad of our children's earthly successes. They are good dancers or singers or athletes; they've received another promotion or been elected to office; they've given us grandchildren. Most of these achievements are reasons to celebrate, yes. But none compares to the deepening spiritual growth we want our children to experience. If we limit our pride to our children's earthly accomplishments, and these are the things they hear us validating in front of others, we may well be sending our children a message—no matter how old they are—that their earthly pursuits are the most important things they are doing in life. That is a pride that threatens to separate our children from the most important priority of life: pursuing God's kingdom and righteousness. Driving that kind of wedge between our children and God is anything but loving!

One last note before we leave these matters of pride and boasting: If you were to devise a wicked plan to drive one of your children into estrangement from you, you could come up with no better idea than to speak exceedingly well of one of your children over another. If we emote favorably about one of our children and offer no such support to the other, we can be sure that the unfavored child will pick up on the difference and run for the affection of someone who does affirm them. Be careful in your boasting about your children, even when it is limited to their spiritual maturity, or you may find that your good words about your daughter create damage to the soul of your son.

When love leads in a relationship—and in the communication that enters that relationship—love sets out to honor the other person.

Love does not dishonor others

The New International Version offers a bit of an extrapolation in its translation of this phrase. The Greek *aschemoneo* points more plainly to rudeness. "[Love] is not rude," the English Standard Version gives us. "[Love] does not act unbecomingly," says the New American Standard. In his paraphrase, The Message, Eugene Peterson puts it this way: "[Love] doesn't force itself on others."

Of course, the inference taken up by the NIV makes sense. When we are rude to others, when we act unbecomingly in their presence, we dishonor them. Love does not rightly do things that are wholly out of place, or that embarrass or demean another.

What does this look like in the practicum of parent-child relationships? Very often, it comes out in criticism, argumentation, or sarcasm. When our children are little, we may readily establish our authority. And while we may employ the rudenesses of a louder voice or a stronger physical presence, our unbecoming ways win out because our children are not equipped to fight back. But as our children grow older, our rudeness is unmasked. They see that we are no bigger or smarter or louder; we are just more boorish. That's a one-ingredient recipe for trouble!

Love, especially because it has the other person in mind, steers clear of the kind of behavior that inevitably creates tension. This does not mean that there is never a time for confrontation, or that seemingly innocent conversations won't ever escalate into real clashes. But when love leads in a relationship—and in the communication that enters that relationship—love sets out to honor the other person. Nit picking? Out. Name calling? Out. Assertions of superiority? Out.

An excellent guideline in walking through minefields with your adult children is to consider how you would approach a similar scenario with your adult colleagues. A firm instruction, an ultimatum, or a censure may be in order. But this is not an open door for demeaning behavior. Direct statements free of personal attacks—these are the hallmark of difficult adult conversations done well. And if your child is established in business, you must recognize that he or she has seen this done well. If, when they find themselves in your presence, they are suddenly fearful of being rudely attacked or demoralized (that is, if they are made to feel like children), they will recognize the difference right now. Your words will be dismissed with a mental "there Dad goes again" or "it's more of the same from Mom." Your child will go to those who honor them, because they have that choice—they are adults!

Among the fruit of the Spirit that Paul listed for the Galatians is kindness. By prayer and petition, get kindness. Get it most of all for your interaction with your adult children. It is the remedy for unloving rudeness. And it comes from the Spirit of God, not from some deeper resolve on your part.

We will love our adult children if we allow them to love and care us as we grow older, but we must continue to guard our hearts against expectations for our children's success that are really tied up in our own emotional or physical or financial needs.

Love is not self-seeking

If parenting is effective at one thing above all, it may be this: exposing our love for ourselves.

In the years of our singleness and romance before we have children, we call the shots. Dinners out, weekend vacations, new clothes, a club membership, even overtime at the office—these were decisions we made with little effect on others. Then along came children, and the sacrifices began. The budget got tighter, sitters weren't available, and we had a pretty good idea that "good parenting" was best measured in time. This is not to say that everyone is willing to make these kinds of sacrifices—some run back to their own life, where they are in charge of the hours and the days. But assuming you were one of those who hung in there, you stepped back from your self-gratifying choices and starting making decisions with the kids in mind. Along the way, you trained your character to be less selfish. In essence, you learned to love by arresting pursuits that were all about you.

Maybe.

Over the past two or three decades, psychologists and sociologists have recognized an increase in parental attention to their children's activities and successes. Where 30 years ago, parents made time to get to their children's school sports activities (for instance) if they could—after the obligations of work were met—now many parents work ways to get off early to see afternoon contests, or travel with their children's teams to special tournaments. In the extreme, some parents have quit their jobs to follow their children to single events, such as the Little League World Series or the Olympic Games. Sure, these are once-in-a-lifetime opportunities and we might argue that a parent who makes such a radical choice is self-sacrificing, but another interpretation is also likely. Many parents live vicariously through their children's achievements. The children may be coming close to fulfilling dreams the parent once had, or they may simply be reaching a level of success the parent never enjoyed. And now, through emotion if nothing else, the parent is experiencing "highs" in life through their child's accomplishments rather than their own.

The danger in this sort of incorporation of another's achievements is a kind of co-dependent success, where the parent gains emotional currency through the child's gains: admission to medical school, election to office, a house at the beach. It is possible that the parent's stake in the child's success drives the parent to push the child harder, or at least to silently yearn for the child's earthly success. There is an extent to which such a desire is biblical—aging parents have traditionally depended on their children to care for them in their later years. But parents of adult children must be very careful not to regress into self-seeking behaviors that cause them to act in demanding, ungrateful fashion. We will love our adult children if we allow them to love and care us as we grow older, but we must continue to guard our hearts against expectations for our children's success that are really tied up in our own emotional or physical or financial needs.

Parents, teachers, and other adults are made legendary by their tirades and rants.

Love is not easily angered

Here is an idea in Paul's writing taken right from the character of God, the definition of which we assessed in chapter two. God is slow to anger; we must be the same.

Impatience turned to anger is one of the most common demonstrations of a tired or exasperated parent. We have all found ourselves in those uncomfortable department store moments when a parent we do not know verbally demeans a child nearby. We may not know exactly what has driven this parent to such a moment, but we recognize the ugliness of emotion and words. In fact, many of us have been this parent—the frustrated one, revealing our wit's ends through fierce eyes and a raised voice.

You must understand that many moments like these are indelibly written on our children's memories. Parents, teachers, and other adults are made legendary by their tirades and rants. Sometimes this is good for a laugh, especially when the fit of anger fits the moment, was rare for this adult, and when the adult was apologetic and self-deprecating. But when a young person becomes a frequent victim of a parent's anger, the injurious consequences live on. As in the well-known analogy of the fence where the nails have been pounded in then extracted, apologies may "remove the nails," but the scars remain. If you were a parent prone to demonstrations of regular or over-the-top anger with your children when they were younger, you may need to be especially sensitive to their approach to you now. They may share space with you tentatively, fearful that you will fall back into those angry fits. You know that Christ has changed you; they are not so sure. If you have met with your children and apologized to them about the anger that you showed before you knew Jesus (or before you surrendered to him in this area of your life), the only remedy going forward is time. You must, by the power of the Holy Spirit, show over years that God has made you new. Trust can be broken in a moment; it takes far longer to rebuild.

Of course, this specific discussion of anger holds weight in several other contexts. If you were known to your children as a gossip, a liar, an unethical business person, a lecher, or a sinner with any particular outstanding sin, you will reestablish trust only by a combination of a sincere, purposed apology in the short-term and a Spirit-infused demonstration of a whole new character and personality in the long-term.

We must recognize that if God's grace covers our sin, and if he removes our transgressions "as far as the east is from the west," then we have no business calling up the sins of others that are bygone and forgiven by God.

Love keeps no record of wrongs

"How many times do I have to tell you?" It is likely one of the most common questions in American parenting, and it is completely rhetorical! In hindsight, we all would have been better parents when our children were small if we had been definitive with our numbers: "I'll give you just *one* more opportunity to get this right, and then we will have to employ consequences for your irresponsibility." Even the youngest

child understands the concept of one! But instead, we fell back onto this old ambiguous saw, simply as a way of venting our exasperation.

Perhaps there is good news here. We might have devised something far worse, something that sounded like this: "Do you realize that is the third time today I have told you to pick up your room? Moreover, I've now told you this fourteen times this week alone, which puts us to 227 times this year, and 1,861 times in your life. No wonder I'm getting tired of this!"

Literally, counting up another's sins sounds absurd. What kind of accountant keeps track of the number of times a person does this thing wrong or that? But records are not made only from numbers. In fact, thousands more people can regenerate in their minds the photograph of Roger Bannister crossing the finish line than can tell you exactly what his time was the day he broke the four-minute mile barrier. Keeping a record may require us to remember only one episode or event.

Love does not replay memories of the ills of others. It is true that some people will harm us over and over in the same way. And we would be foolish to allow them to continue abusing us, either by their words or their actions. Our God is a strong tower; we should run to him for safety when others come to harm us. But apart from this, we must recognize that if God's grace covers our sin, and if he removes our transgressions "as far as the east is from the west" (Psalm 103:12), then we have no business calling up the sins of others that are bygone and forgiven by God. In fact, if by reminding our children of their sins, we convey to them that we have not yet forgiven them, we bring ourselves under the condemnation of Matthew 6:15: "But if you do not forgive others their sins, your Father will not forgive your sins."

Certainly, as a parent, you have an intimate perspective of your child, even into their adulthood. This means that you may see their weaknesses as readily as anyone other than their own spouse or children. But here is where it is especially important to remind yourself that your child is an adult, and that you wouldn't dare make a habit of pointing out the past sins of other adults. Stop, let the gospel do its redeeming work, and let your trust for your child be rebuilt in love as God works in the life of your child in the same way that he is working in your life.

Love simply cannot accept choices and actions that threaten others.

Love does not delight in evil

On the surface, this may seem like the most obvious of Paul's statements about love. We would never want to see evil come to those we love. And yet…

In an age where tolerance and love are often coupled together, it is a commonly accepted thought that we would not keep those we love from doing things that they enjoy. Those who understand God's desires for our earthly lives, however, recognize that activities enjoyed by the flesh are too often harmful to the person who engages in them, and possibly detrimental to others as well. In fact, recognition of God is not required for recognition of evil. We have all crossed paths with non-religious friends whose past includes the entrapment of addiction. These friends speak of "the demons" of alcohol or drug abuse. When pressed, they may say that their understanding of demonic activity is more literary than spiritual, yet they will go on to confirm the evil nature of addiction because they have fallen victim to such consequences as criminal activity (such as driving while intoxicated or public fighting), separation or divorce, job loss, and poverty.

Love simply cannot accept choices and actions that threaten others in this way. It does not laugh off casual drunkenness, in the same way that it does not champion sexual promiscuity or unethical business schemes or hurtful words—all of which harm not only the actor but those acted upon. When adult children want you to allow for such actions, you may recognize that this is the way of the person who is not in Christ (1 Corinthians 5:9-10), but in love and with a loving tone you will speak against these self-scarring actions. You would speak this way if you saw a friend going down such roads; you may speak with love-laced warning to your adult children, too.

When you see your son or daughter—maybe both!—turning their eyes in Jesus' direction, encourage their further seeking, even if some of their current insights don't quite line up with mainstream Christian thinking.

Love rejoices in the truth

It is easy to like the way that Eugene Peterson helps us understand the gold in this little phrase of Paul's. In *The Message*, Peterson renders this line: "[Love] takes pleasure in the flowering of truth."

When we are frustrated, even tired, from the interaction we have with adult children who do not show any interest in the will of God for their lives, we can fall into a kind of fatalism that rarely allows us to see positives in their lives. But if we fail to notice the flowering of truth in our children's lives, we miss one of the best opportunities we have to affirm in them just what we have been hoping to see.

In their book, *The Shaping of Things to Come*, Michael Frost and Alan Hirsch discuss the phenomenon that while some people may be "in" with God—they've prayed a prayer of salvation and hung around the church—they may in fact be moving away from God's will for their life by the way they think, speak, and act. Meanwhile, we might find many still "on the outside"—no definitive commitment yet to Christ— who are earnestly investigating matters of faith in Jesus. They are asking thoughtful questions and may even be adopting some of the practices of the Christian walk in order to give them a test.[1]

As a parent who has not given up on love for your adult child, you do not want to overlook these kinds of directional changes in your child's life. When you see your son or daughter—maybe both!—turning their eyes in Jesus' direction, encourage their further seeking, even if some of their current insights don't quite line up with mainstream Christian thinking. Find the truth in what they are saying and affirm it. And while you may want to temper your rejoicing in front of your child, don't hold back in thanking the Lord for these "baby steps" in your adult child. Ask him for more of the same, until your children have given their whole heart to Jesus.

What we must want for our children is what God wants for our children: their hearts given over to him.

Love always protects

Paul incorporated five absolute statements in closing his "love list" to the Corinthians—four things that love should always do and one thing that it should never do. Obviously, we might throw up our hands at this point and cry, "Impossible!" Honestly, this is what God would have us do. For it is when we come to the end of our own attempts at getting it all right that we learn to rely completely on him. When Jesus told the disciples that it is easier for a camel to pass through the eye of a needle than for a wealthy person to enter the kingdom of heaven, they asked him who then could possibly be saved. Jesus replied, "With man this is impossible, but with God all things are possible" (Matthew 19:26). Perhaps if there is a core encouragement we can give you in this book it is this:

Take heart. Rely on God. Through him all things are possible. He doesn't even need your help!

Let's go ahead and look, then, at one of those absolutes that God can do in perfecting his love in you.

It should be clear by now that we mean it when we say that part of loving others is hating the things that would harm them. This means that we will do all we can to keep friends, including our adult children, from the influences and temptations that would draw their heart away from God. We cannot emphasize that last phrase enough! We are not protecting our children for our sake—for our pleasure or pride or comfort. We are not protecting them from ungodly options so that others will affirm our parenting prowess. What we must want for our children is what God wants for our children: their hearts given over to him.

This leads to two important understandings.

First, while we will inform our friends of what God wants for our lives in an effort to influence their chasing after him, we cannot leap in between them and every temptation that comes their way. Indeed, earthly consequences of sinful living are often the very thing that opens one's eyes to the weight and effect of their sin. When Paul wrote to the Corinthians that they should hand an incestuous "brother" among them to "over to Satan…so that his spirit may be saved on the day of the Lord," he meant this very thing. What we are saying is this: we must include among our protective acts on behalf of our adult children a protection against the deception that tells them their sinful living is no big deal. Allowing for the natural consequences of a person's sin is part of this kind of protection. It should never be our earliest attempt at helping a child—that first approach should be direct, clear instruction—but it is an approach we may move to when the sin is repeated and/or escalated.

Second, we must recognize that one of the things from which we may have to protect our children is ourselves. There are some parents whose emotional investment is so great, or whose spiritual maturity in areas like patience and teaching is not advanced, so that they must defer to others to speak into their children's lives. Pray for other voices to captivate your adult children—voices that reflect the voice of God himself.

What we might say generally, and ironically, is that this absolute—as well as those to come—requires balance. Loving protection may not always be practiced best as we might think to practice it at first blush. When it comes to applying an absolute, we are smart to keep in mind Paul's exhortation to the Philippians that they "work out [their] salvation with fear and trembling"—that is, to apply your life in Christ by always consulting Christ and submitting to the leading of his Spirit.

If your children have broken trust with you so that you would be unwise to give them responsibility in certain matters, express to them that you do not want this condition to last; you are willing to work with them to rebuild trust between you.

Love always trusts

Here we find ourselves in another tangle. Always trust? Even when we have been hurt again and again by the sinful, self-serving choices of others?

Many adult children abuse their parents. They do so by working their way into deep trouble and expecting their parents to bail them out—with an always-available bedroom or no-strings-attached financial help. Again and again parents may respond as requested and repeatedly adult children go into the desert of their sin and lay expectations on the oasis that is their parents' stability. In cases like these, a parent's trust understandably erodes. Some parents hold out longer than others, but there is wisdom in the old axiom: "Fool me once, shame on you. Fool me twice, shame on me."

And yet…Paul wrote "forgive as the Lord forgave you" (Colossians 3:13).

And yet…Jesus explained to Peter that he should be lavish in his forgiveness—"seventy times seven" times.

And yet…Jesus told the parable of the prodigal son, received joyfully back into his home.

But let's recognize that this same parable teaches that forgiveness and a reinstatement of trust are not the same thing. The father in the parable welcomes his wayward son with open arms, throwing a party for his returning adult child. You are probably familiar with the story and know that the father's celebration does not sit well with the older brother. But in our (rightful) criticism of the older brother's gripes, we often miss this promise of the father to the older son: "My son, you are always with me, and everything I have is yours" (Luke 15:31). The father did not plan to carve up the older brother's inheritance and give half of it to the returning son, who had already taken his inheritance and squandered it on "wild living." Certainly, part of the father's intention was to act equitably between his sons. But another part had to have in mind the fact that the younger son could not at this stage of his life be trusted with cash in hand. The father was prepared to provide an avenue of work for his younger son, a way to make a living and a home, but he felt no obligation to hand him more of his own money when his son's recent life demonstrated irresponsibility and disregard for the value of money.

So what could Paul mean when he says that "love always trusts"? Let us suggest three things.

First, he means that we should always be looking for ways to trust others, including our adult children. A person who is untrustworthy in one regard may be trustworthy in other regards. For instance, while most people will attempt to cover their unwise tracks with lies and stories, others are always wholly truthful when confronted with their ill choices. God called David a man after God's own heart even though David would go on to commit several "big sins." How could this be? David, though sinful, readily admitted his sins when confronted and earnestly sought restoration with God. Find the ways that your children can be trusted and increase your levels of trust in these areas.

Second, we should always emphasize forgiveness. When we do this, we may tell our adult children that while we cannot yet trust them in various matters, we have forgiven them and we want to move toward the restoration of our relationship with them, including the day when we may trust them again. We *want* to trust our adult children, just as we want to trust everyone we encounter. But trust is gained over time, and regained over more time. If your children have broken trust with you so that you would be unwise to give them responsibility in certain matters, express to them that you do not want this condition to last; you are willing to work with them to rebuild trust between you.

Third and certainly most important, we should always trust God on our children's behalf. We should appeal to the Lord, asking for him to draw our children closer to him, whether they now profess to be walking with him or not. If this is our real desire for our adult children—that they would grow in their relationship with God and demonstrate their reverence for him through their actions—then we need to act on this desire in faith and trust ourselves.

When two parties are seeking God's kingdom and righteousness, there is an increasingly excellent chance that the relationship between them will become intimate, guided by the Holy Spirit.

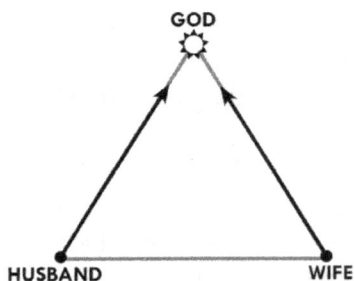

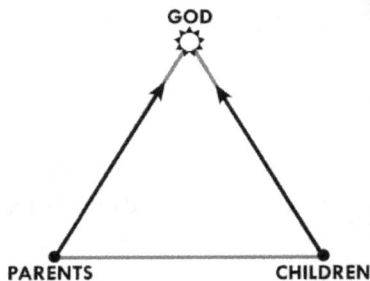

Love always hopes
You do not need us to tell you that you are reading this book because you hope that the relationship you have with your adult children may become a relationship where the pursuit you and your children share in common is the pursuit of a richer life in Jesus. You have likely seen the oft-shared picture of a Christ-focused marriage. When the husband and wife are both pursing Christ above all things (as opposed to pursuing one another) and looking to draw nearer to him, they inevitably draw nearer to one another. We can create a similar picture for parents and children. When both parties are seeking God's kingdom and righteousness, there is an increasingly excellent chance that the relationship between them will become intimate, guided by the Holy Spirit.

GOD
☼

HUSBAND   WIFE

GOD
☼

PARENTS   CHILDREN

If parenting goes on until the day we are united with Jesus, then our love for our children should be infused with hope. In his letter to the Romans, Paul wrote that we do not hope for what we already have. If the refrigerator is full, we don't hope that a delivery person will show up at our door with another week of groceries! Instead, we hope for what we do not yet have—though we know it is coming—and we wait patiently for this hope to be fulfilled (Romans 8:24-25). What you may find fascinating here is that the hope that our children will grow closer and closer to Jesus is a hope we maintain even when our children are walking with the Lord. Their sanctification is just like ours; in Christ, our lives are always "under construction." So we hope and pray that our children are increasingly surrendering their hearts to Jesus as each day passes.

Loving, faith-filled perseverance is measured in two ways: prayer and longevity.

Love always perseveres

A love that hopes flows naturally into a love that perseveres. In the same Romans 8 passage where Paul wrote of waiting patiently for hope, he began by writing of the groaning that goes on in our spirit as we wait for God's work to be done. Hope will not always come easily. Sometimes, the best faith we can have is a stubborn faith, a faith that holds on when there seems to be no evidence other than that faith. Indeed, you have probably read this well-known passage in the book of Hebrews: "Faith is confidence of what we hope for and assurance about what we do not see." The evidence is not in the seeing, but in the knowing—knowing that God is faithful and trustworthy.

Loving, faith-filled perseverance is measured in two ways: prayer and longevity.

When we remain faithful in prayer, we motivate God's answer. Jesus told the parable of a man who knocked on his friend's home past midnight, asking for some bread for his houseguests. The man in bed did not respond simply because he was his neighbor's friend but rather, Jesus said, because the man was persistent (or bold) with his knocking. It was in this context that Jesus notably said, "Ask and it will be given to you; seek and you will find; knock and the door will be opened to you. For everyone who asks receives; the one who seeks finds, and to the one who knocks, the door will be opened" (Luke 11:9-10). Hope is best expressed to God in our time of prayer with him. And the fullness of our desire is best demonstrated by our consistent requests in prayer.

While longevity applies in prayer, it may also apply in life. Though it is painful for us, the answers to our parental prayers may not come until after we ourselves have gone to be with Jesus. I (JC) had an uncle whose conversion—for which his mother had prayed for many, many years—did not come until after she died. In fact, it was at her funeral, when he was confronted with the godly nature of his mother's life, that my uncle recognized his need for this same kind of relationship with Jesus. By this time my uncle was in his fifties, but there was no less rejoicing in heaven at his salvation than if he had come as a small child—indeed, there may have been more, for his mother was there to celebrate with the angels!

Understand that your perseverance may be frequently coupled with tears. Some days the line between disappointment and hope is very fine indeed. There is a reason *patience* is also translated *long-suffering* in many Bibles! But if your tears and anguish represent the love you have for your child, you are on the right path.

We are meant to be a people whose motion is Godward;
we know that he is waiting to draw near to us.

Love never fails

Finally, we reach the absolute that we have chosen for the title of this book. Love, we are told in various translations, "never fails," "never ends," "will last forever," "never dies." There is a thread God has woven through eternity, from its "beginning" to its "end." That thread is love. It begins with God. And when we catch hold of it, really have it in hand by way of God's Son, then it will last in us as well. The fact that love does not die is the very reason that we parent until we do.

Before we move forward, we want to encourage you to do all you can to cultivate your own love for God. James gave us such an encouragement when he wrote: "Come near to God and he will come near to you" (James 4:8). We are meant to be a people whose motion is Godward; we know that he is waiting to draw near to us. If, as John wrote, "we love because he first loved us" (1 John 4:19), then we want to get close to God and lay hold of as much of his love as possible. We're going to need it—because through the natural intimacy we have with our children, we are in a greater position to be hurt by their disrespect and irresponsibility and selfishness and godlessness than by any other person except our spouse. But when we have God's love, we have all we need to think rightly about others, demonstrate God's grace for them, and anticipate Jesus' work of salvation in their hearts.

Honestly, without Jesus, you can throw the rest of this book away. Your ability to offer anything of lasting value to your children hinges totally on him. So does your desire to see them made right with God. You must have Jesus.

4 NOT EASY TO LOVE

CAN WE LET YOU in on a secret? The last chapter blew us away, too. When you read 1 Corinthians 13 with a mind for taking its words seriously, where you find yourself is in a place of inadequacy. You feel utterly incapable of ever loving like *that*—or at least not up to the task today.

That feeling of ineptitude when it comes to love is one part *us*; we know our own weaknesses and shortcomings, and we aren't so sure we want to take on this task of loving like Jesus. Even as parents of adult children, we recognize that we have so much growing up to do. We know that we are supposed to rely on the Holy Spirit to bring us to a place where we can even attempt to rightly obey God, but most of us are more familiar with our weaknesses than with the Holy Spirit's strength. God is still working in us.

But that feeling is a second part *them*; we know our children's weaknesses and shortcomings too, and we know how their words and actions have disappointed and disturbed us in ways to which they are wholly blind. Simply put, they have often made themselves hard to love.

Enter C.S. Lewis. In his classic apologetic work, *Mere Christianity*, Lewis considered what it means to keep on loving someone whose life is not lovable:

> I used to think this a silly, straw-splitting distinction: how could you hate what a man did and not hate the man? But years later it occurred to me that there was one man to whom I had been doing this all my life—namely myself. However much I might dislike my own cowardice or conceit or greed, I went on loving myself. There had never been the slightest difficulty about it. In fact the very reason why I hated the things was that I loved the man. Just because I loved myself, I was sorry to find that I was the sort of man who did those things.[2]

It is not impossible to love our children when they act unlovably any more than it is impossible to love our ugly selves. So we persist in our love even when it is difficult.

For this reason, we want to spend time in this chapter putting together a pattern for loving our children, addressing the matter of *applying our love*, the fourth key idea listed in chapter two.

In a way, the pattern of love is progressive, moving from one step or phase to another. But if we are not regularly doubling back and refreshing our attention to the early steps, we will lose the ground we have gained along the way.

A new life is possible

It would surprise us that you have read this far in a book so laced with scriptural references if you have not committed to a life in Jesus Christ. However, many people spend a lifetime "kicking the tires" in a religious fashion without ever "buying the car," so to speak. In Jesus' own day, there were plenty of people who came and went, fascinated by his miracles or interested in how he engaged the religious leaders of the time; but when the call to follow Jesus wholeheartedly came their way, they began to think of obligations and excuses (see Luke 9:57-62).

So we're going to ask you plainly: where do you stand with Jesus?

The Bible across its pages illuminates the fact that while God is holy, we forsook his holiness in an effort to rule our own lives. This is not only the story of Adam and Eve, or the story of "all mankind." This is the story of each one us, who must say with C.S. Lewis (and the apostle Paul!) that our lives bear all the damning evidence necessary to separate us from God for eternity. Knowing this, however, God planned our salvation, announcing its coming through the words of the prophets. Through the line of Abraham and Isaac and Jacob, and Ruth and Boaz and David and Solomon, into the home of Joseph the carpenter through the womb of Mary the virgin, Jesus was born, the incarnation (physical embodiment) of God himself.

Jesus' life *was* full of miracles. These signs and wonders accredited him to those who saw him, walked with him, and would carry forward the account of his life, death and resurrection. As the one perfect sacrifice, Jesus shed his blood on a Roman cross to make atonement for our sins, once and for all. Then, after he was buried in a wealthy man's tomb, he arose from this horrible death, just as he had prophesied. In these acts he had broken the power of sin and death; he had made a way—the only perfect way acceptable to God—for salvation.

The good news, then, is that we do not have to make a way for ourselves. Not only is every attempt at righteousness apart from faith in Jesus onerous and exhausting, all of those efforts produce increasing frustration that ends short of the mark. We are simply incapable of bridging the gap between our unholy thoughts and motives and words and actions and the God who is completely awe-inspiring in his holiness. His eternal dwelling is without flaw, and if we were to attempt to enter it in our righteous disguises (even religious ones!) we would be thrown out as pretenders.

But the best news is that we can ride the coattails of the one who got it all right: Jesus. The Bible says that those who confess with their mouth that Jesus is Lord and believe in their hearts that God raised him from the dead will be saved. More than that, they become "joint heirs" to the kingdom of God with Jesus himself. In Christ, we are picked up and moved from one way of life—lived according to our own rules and depending on our own efforts—to another life—lived by the power of the Spirit of God now in us.

Honestly, without Jesus, you can throw the rest of this book away. Your ability to offer anything of lasting value to your children hinges totally on him. So does your desire to see them made right with God. You must have Jesus.

It's okay if this not an easy decision for you. Jesus himself said that we should consider the cost before following him. If you surrender to him as he is asking, this will have an effect on your life. It may have some very big effects—odd looks from your friends, the loss of business partners, additional time and attention to your marriage and family. But when you go into your relationship with Jesus knowing that these changes will come, starting with your own view of life, you will be willing to stick with your commitment, with confirmation in your spirit that it is the right way to go. (If you need more time to study and reflect on who Jesus is and what he looks for from us, we recommend that you work your way through the Scriptures outlined in our Links Players Bible study, "Jesus – Savior, Lord, Treasure," available as a free pdf download at http://linksplayers.com/Resources/Bible_Studies/Jesus_Savior_Lord_Treasure.pdf.)

If you are now ready for the first time in your life to definitively say "yes" to Jesus, knowing that what he has done for you is unobtainable anywhere else, you may pray this prayer: "Lord God in heaven, I have missed your perfect mark with all my attempts, both religious and irreligious. What I really need is someone who will rescue me from my sin. What I would really like is someone who can clear an avenue for me to build a life with you. I believe that Jesus is this person. He is the Savior and I want to make him my Lord today. I've been a slave to sin all my life; now I want to be a willing, committed servant of the one who loved me so much that he died on the cross for me. Lord, take my life and make it new. Make me a person of faith in you and you alone."

Admitting your mistakes

Entering into a relationship with Jesus often begins by recognizing and admitting our mistakes. We are not perfect people—not even close. But when we are willing to confess our sin to God, we find that a weight we have been carrying is lifted from our spirit. This is an ongoing process, actually. The Holy Spirit, working with us to become more like Christ in our walk with him, gently but pointedly reveals sin in our thoughts and emotions, as well as in the things we actually say and do. Then we find ourselves confessing our sin again, deepening the connection between God and ourselves.

But the recognition and admission of sin is not something God wants us to do only with him. In the Sermon on the Mount, Jesus cut through our religion with this statement: "If you are offering your gift at the altar and there remember that your brother or sister has something against you, leave your gift there in front of the altar. First go and be reconciled to them; then come and offer your gift" (Matthew 5:23-24). Jesus' brand of religion kept pushing for humble transparency. All the religious acts in the world mean nothing if your heart is not right with God and with others.

Authority almost inevitably breeds pride. When one is granted a superior position over others, it does not take long for the one on top to perceive all their ideas and plans as better than those of the people below them. Pride takes hold. Parents are not immune to this. From the day our children are born, we are in charge. We occupy the superior position. And as the years progress and our children are emboldened to counter our perspective on any number of issues, we feel threatened. *How could such a good idea come from such a little snot?* we catch ourselves thinking when we contend with a child, and thus we dismiss the fact that he or she is maturing before our eyes. By this process, we find ourselves guarding our superiority as a matter of pride—because we are *the parents*. Really, could we dream up any more effective way to embitter our children, especially as they move into adulthood?

Such pride is the very thing God is trying to kill in us. He will have none of it if we are to grow in him. It is the humble whom he lifts up (James 4:10).

We need to take a good look at our parental roles, then. While you may have been a very good parent most of the time, if you are unwilling to see faults and errors in your parenting, you will be missing what your children have seen in you. And if you miss what they see in you—the place where your pride has stuck for no good reason—then the chasm between you and your children will deepen.

We fill gaps between us and others by confessing our sins to one another and seeking forgiveness. You can imagine how important this is between those who are closest, those who have had the most potential for and practice in hurting each other.

A meeting of transparency

In order to let your adult children know that you are now cognizant of the mistakes you have made in parenting through the years, you will likely need to arrange a meeting of transparency. Call your child and say, "There is something I need to talk to you about." If they are hesitant, continue, "It's all about me, things that I am seeing in the way I live my life that I do not like. Will you sit down with me and let me explain?" After getting past the shock of hearing you say these words, they may agree to such a meeting.

Now set a place and time. In your mind, for your child's sake, set a specific limit on the time you will take as well. This meeting has the potential for being very emotional. That is fine. If the emotion between you causes the meeting to run over your designated timeframe, let it do so. What you're trying to prevent by planning a time limit is your own rambling on. This is about you and your confession—but that is certainly not all it is about! It is much more about restoring relationship with your adult child. You have to be prepared to allow them to respond.

If you have to travel for this meeting, we suggest that you plan to stay in the area at least 24 hours after the meeting. Upon first hearing you out, your child may need time to reflect on what you have said, some time to process whether you are "for real." If you both live in the same city or region, a follow-up meeting may be easily arranged. But if you live geographically separated from your children, allowing some time for a second meeting is wise.

In any case, you must keep in mind that your speaking is only as valuable as your adult children's listening—their actually hearing you. For this to happen best, you are going to have to allow them to determine and exercise their level and parameters of comfort.

- What if you have more than one child with whom you need to meet?

You will have to consider each of your children and where they are in their own life, particularly their life with God. You are about to explain to your children that God is changing your heart; he is the one who has motivated you to talk honestly with them and to seek their forgiveness. Some children will be utterly resistant to such talk. Others may have already beaten you to the Jesus punch—they will delight in what you have to tell them. You also need to consider how your children relate to one another. If they are normally contentious with one another, you do not want to attempt to unite them by meeting together with them—they may disagree with what you have to tell them just to spite one another! In some cases, you may find it acceptable to meet with more than one of your children together; more often, meeting with them individually will make the best sense.

- What if your children don't want to meet with you?

If you have been estranged from one or more of your children for some time, it is possible—even likely—that they will not want to meet with you. Disrespect remains in your child toward you. This may be the child's own perspective, a condition of sin in their own heart. However, disrespect of that sort usually fades after the teenage years. The old saying generally holds true: "The older I get, the smarter my dad (or mom) gets." However, where a child has been hurt by a parent's own sin, the disrespect that child possesses toward the parent(s) may have a basis. Yes, the child would be greatly aided by forgiving the parent; but this will almost always follow a parent's own confession of sin and admission of the hurt that has been caused.

If your child does not want to meet with you, then, you must begin by asking yourself whether this lack of interest in repairing the relationship emerges from hurt that you have caused your child and for which you have not sought forgiveness. Are you willing to humble yourself and admit what you have done wrong? If not, you will need to spend time talking to God before you talk to your child. Confess your specific sins to God and ask him to prepare you to do the same with your children.

If, on the other hand, you have made numerous attempts to "bring the prodigal home" with forgiveness and grace through the years and your child still does not want to meet with you, you will... need to talk to God. Though your circumstances are different, the remedy is the same! Ask the Lord to soften your child's heart and to open avenues for his or her return to a place where the two of you can sit and talk.

You may also need to recognize that while God calls you to do the right thing, you cannot always be responsible for the reactions of others. Paul wrote to the Romans: "If it is possible, as far as it depends on you, live at peace with everyone" (Romans 12:18). There are times when living at peace with others will not be possible, because the estrangement does not depend on you. You have prayerfully, faithfully, lovingly made every attempt to reopen the lines of conversation between you and your child and—so far—your prayers have not been answered. May we give you the one encouragement we have left? Be faithful and full of hope. God has not yet written the end of your story, or your child's.

- What should you say?
If we could, we would script an ideal conversation for you

when you finally have the opportunity to sit down with your adult child and explain what God has done in your life. But there are no ideal conversations. And each of us has our own natural way of saying things, according to our own personality and the language we are used to using. This doesn't mean we can't offer some important guidelines, but recognize that you should feel free to choose the words that work best for you, as long as you speak openly and mercifully.

To begin, you must apologize. This should be the chief purpose of your meeting. In fact, you may use this as the pretext for your getting together when you first talk to your son or daughter, saying something like, "I'd really like to meet with you. There are some changes I am making in my life and I want you to know about them, because I recognize some mistakes I have made, and I want to be sure that I am in good standing with you."

Then, when you are sitting down together, don't hem and haw. Get right to the point. Apologize specifically and directly for errors that you have made that have contributed to pain or difficulty in your child's life and a broken relationship between you. Apologize as well for any lack of love, guidance and encouragement that you have demonstrated through the years. Convey to your child that you are taking responsibility for the holes in your relationship, caused either or both by your godless actions or your irresponsibility in leading your home spiritually as you now know you should have. You do not need to go "over the top" here, apologizing for things you did not do, but you must also realize that you may be apologizing for the perceptions of your children as much as for your actions. This is okay. Finally, you may apologize for the fact that the two of you simply have not been able to "connect" through the years, and then state that you greatly desire a renewed relationship with your child.

Second, speak personally about the things God has done in your life. You do not need to speak like a theologian and you don't want to turn preachy! You simply want to say what you can about the things you have learned about Jesus' salvation, and about God's lordship in your life. Keep the focus on you personally, rather than on church, religion, or the need for the "whole world" to do the same. Just tell the story of what God is doing in your life.

Third, explain how you want things to be different in your life and in your family, again with the emphasis on you. You may talk about things God is teaching you through the Scriptures, particularly about love and forgiveness. You may draw lines back to your mistakes here, explaining it like this: "I know that I have been a boorish, often mean, person through the years. And I know that my example turned you away. I am sorry for that. I believe God is changing me in my heart, and I have asked him to change my words and actions in this area. Honestly, I want to reflect God in a way that people, but especially you, can see. I want to be patient, gentle, helpful, and encouraging with my words. I know from what you have seen of me before, this might seem impossible, but that is honestly what I want. I know now that there is no way I can do this on my own, so I am trusting God to do it for me."

Finally, a word about what not to say, which is easier to achieve if we remember that the whole point here is for this meeting to be the first of many. Do not prod your child. Do not give advice. This may sound self-centered when we say it this way, but this first meeting is about you. It is about what you recognize having done wrong in the way you have lived around your child (as a person but also as a parent), and it is about explaining that by God's grace you do not intend to live that way any longer. You are asking your child to forgive you—though we do not recommend that you push for such forgiveness in this meeting. Many children will need time to see whether this change in you is real before they are ready to forgive you. Asking them to forgive you during this meeting is placing the pressure on *them*. If you really want to display love to your child, let all the weight of this meeting fall on *you*. Your child has likely done a lot of squirming already just to agree to sit down with you! If you are truly willing to let God do his work in your life, let it be evident in the way you conduct the course of this meeting.

Which leads to one last note here: the one conducting the course of the meeting, if you will let him, is God. Both Jesus and Peter spoke of the Holy Spirit supplying the necessary words when we are speaking to others of our faith. We have said that, though an adult, your child will be squirming at a meeting such as this. No doubt, you will be nervous yourself. Paul wrote to the Philippians that they should not "worry about anything, but instead pray about everything" (Philippians 4:6, TLB). Go into this meeting prayerfully. Go into it fully dependent on God. Go into it ready to watch God do his excellent work! The title of this chapter is "Not Easy to Love." Here is one of those situations that may be exceedingly difficult for you. But wonder of wonders, it is also one of those situations that can build your budding faith.

Praying strategically for your children

After reading this far into this book, you may be reeling from the breadth of work to be done between you and your adult children. It is tempting when we feel crushed by the weight of damaged relationships or broken communication to simply throw up our hands and declare the matter "impossible." Then we stop working at making things happen, falling into a sort of fatalistic détente. Our conversations narrow and take on a cautionary politeness, because it can be very difficult to spend extended time with people who do not share the most important beliefs and values in our lives. This is true even among secular families, where politics or social expectations take precedence.

A chapter ago, we looked at the well-known passage where Jesus told his disciples, "With God, all things are possible." We have nearly all encountered this line before, but few of us manage to keep it in mind during the most daunting circumstances in our lives, when our judgment is clouded by the personal nature of the difficulty. Yet its words are as potent as any we will read—if we dare to believe them.

The necessary response to such a truth is the same now as it has always been: cry out to God in prayer. When we read the pages of Scripture and see how people vigorously entreated God, we should find ourselves moved to follow their examples and begin praying (you might particularly consider Hannah's prayer in 1 Samuel 1 and the prayer of Hezekiah in 2 Kings 20).

How shall we pray? Here are several suggestions for strengthening and structuring your prayers for your adult children:

Pray in faith
In James 1, we read that our prayers must be requests filled with faith. While many people believe this is the most necessary aspect of prayer, they resist praying boldly. This mistake is normally the result of judging our own faith. We think we are too weak to pray with great faith. But faith should never be placed in ourselves or our faith. Faith must be placed in God. Do you believe in God? Do you believe that he is capable of working a miracle—especially the miracle of repentance and salvation—in your adult child's life? If so, your faith is rightly based on the power of God. There will be times when

Praying strategically for your adult children

- Pray in faith
- Pray regularly
- Pray specifically
- Pray for the influences in your child's life

you need to return to some of the great passages of Scripture about God himself in order to remind yourself that this is your God, the God of all creation and holiness (passages like Zephaniah 3:17, Luke 4:14-21, Colossians 1:15-23, and Hebrews 4:14-16). When your faith is based on his nature and his promises, you will be able to set out in prayer, knowing that he is hearing you.

This kind of faith-filled prayer is also necessary if we are to accept the answers that appear before our eyes. You may, for instance, experience increased animosity from your adult children, even though you are stepping up your commitment to pray for them. They may fall deeper into the unrighteous acts of sin. But if our prayers have been placed in God's hands—and are not dependent on our faith or our limited view of time—then we will be encouraged to trust him for his answer, even if that answer appears delayed or skewed. In fact, we must not fail to mention that some people are told by God in response to a prayer they have offered, "I will handle this. Trust me." In that case, to go on praying as if this promise had not been given would be to pray with a lack of trust, as though we will be heard because of our many words (Matthew 6:7). What you may pray instead is this: "Lord, thank you for your promise to answer my prayer. Make me increasingly strong to trust you as I wait to see that answer."

Pray regularly
In light of what we have just written, it may seem counterintuitive now to emphasize the need to keep approaching God over matters of our heart, including matters concerning our

adult children. One reason we must encourage you to "keep the prayers coming," however, is that many people do not receive a definitive promise from the Lord. Therefore, they do well to adhere to the principle of praying perseverance that Jesus taught through the parable of the persistent widow in Luke 18. Here, Jesus praised the woman who continually pleaded her case with a local judge. The judge finally agreed to hear her case because of her relentless appeals. Then Jesus said that God would do the same for those who "cry out to him day and night."

As often as your child makes an impression on your heart, you should be praying. And even when your child has hurt you again and your heart's own desire is to protect itself from more of this pain by shutting its door to your child, pray all the same. In the same way that you are praying for your child's heart to be softened toward God, pray that your heart would not be hardened to your child. Keeping the door of prayer open is vital to keeping the door of your heart open to your child, so that you may render love and compassion as the Holy Spirit guides you to do.

Pray specifically
What do you want God to do?

Hannah wanted a child, Hezekiah his life.

When a blind man called out to Jesus, the Lord asked him, "What do you want me to do for you?"

"Rabbi, I want to see!" Bartimaeus responded (Mark 10:51).

Do not fall into the lazy pattern of saying only, "Lord, I pray for Jonathan." Rather, tell the Lord what you want to see happen in your child: "Lord, you know that Jonathan is making choices to run from you. Would you grab his heart and turn him to you? Would you save him? How overjoyed I would be if my son would give his life to you. You've rescued me; please, rescue him."

Pray for the influences in your child's life
Your adult children are surrounded by people each day who have the ability to influence them in numerous ways. In fact, if you attempted to raise your child as a believer in Jesus from an early age and he or she chose to go another direction, the likely beginning of that choice came through the influence of others. We all have a proclivity for finding people who encourage the choices our sinful natures most want to make—addicts, we know, find camaraderie among other addicts.

But this kind of influence does not have to be negative in every context. I (JH) worked many summers for a camp director who would often sell parents on the value of Christian camping with this line: "The things you have been telling your child all year long sound brand new when coming from a counselor." How true! Likewise, our adult children reject many of the things that we want to say to them about Jesus and faith in him for one key reason: we are the ones saying those things. The words are coming from those "same old folks." We would do well, then, to pray that the Lord would bring into our children's lives the kind of influences that would pique their interest, provide a solid Christ-honoring example, and make clear the Good News of Jesus. If the Holy Spirit is the one who truly leads any of us to Jesus, then he is also the one who leads to us the people who are instrumental in living out and laying out the message of God's grace and salvation. Make a habit of praying for such people to show up in the lives of your children and to speak the living word of God to them. (In the closing chapter of this book, where Jeffrey Cranford tells his own story, you will hear of an influence like this that made a key difference at a key time in his life.)

Impact of a quiet life

Stop for a few minutes now to think about someone who has made a significant impression on you over time. Call this person to mind and begin to reflect on the things about this person that have been particularly meaningful or influential to you. You might even jot down several of these characteristics and push yourself to remember two or three more. Now here is an interesting question: Did you write down anything that this person has specifically said to you? Or are your thoughts and notes exclusively reflective of the way the person goes about his or her life?

Certainly we are not trying to discount the good advice this person has given to you through the years, or the meaningful bits of encouragement, or even the power of the story of their upbringing as they have told it to you. If we asked you to write down several of the excellent pieces of instruction or philosophy that your friend or mentor has given to you, it is likely that you would come up with some spoken words that have stuck with you and guided your own life choices. But here's the point: When we look at the qualities of a person whose life we desire to emulate, we nearly always list characteristics and behaviors before words. And yet, we spend large amounts of time worrying about what exactly we might say to our adult children to convince them to come to Jesus or live in a way more pleasing to him!

When the apostle Paul wrote to one of his favorite churches, the Thessalonians, he painted a picture of a compelling life. Look: "Make it your ambition to lead a quiet life: You should mind your own business and work with your hands, just as we told you, so that your daily life may win the respect of outsiders and so that you will not be dependent on anybody" (1 Thessalonians 4:11-12). There's no jibber-jabber in this picture, no soapboxing, no politicking. What wins the respect of people, especially those who are "outsiders" to the faith in Christ, is a life humbly and righteously lived.

What this means is that the way you live your life in front of your adult children may be the most important thing you ever "say" to them. This is especially true if you came to Jesus later in your own life after living in a way that had nothing to do with him and everything to do with you. If what your children grew up seeing in you was someone they recognized as self-centered, arrogant, loud-mouthed, angry, career-driven, addictive, demanding, promiscuous, intemperate, lazy, rash, or foolish (we have to end the list somewhere), what they need to see in you now—more than anything—is someone who has been changed by the power of God. This takes time. In fact, in many cases, it takes at least as long as that previous time in your life did. (Remember, one of the great attributes of love is patience.)

Consider the nature of trust. Trust, while taking any number of repeated positive instances to build up, can be completely broken in just one act. That is, though you may have spoken truthfully to your child an all occasions but one, if that one lie is uncovered and hurtful to your child, he or she may have great difficulty ever fully trusting you again. And even if the lie was intended more as a cover-up from another person (your spouse, for instance), if your child became aware of the falsehood behind your words, he or she will fight doubts about many other things you have said. Moreover, emotionally charged events like affairs and divorces, criminal acts (especially those resulting in jail time), or embarrassing public incidents such as fits of rage or ugly drunkenness all create partitions of distrust between you and your children. And the effects of this distrust linger well into adulthood, if not for a lifetime. Even if your child forgives you, the scars evidenced by distrust remain.

One of the greatest difficulties for redeemed adults comes when they recognize, like the man we discussed in the opening lines of this book, how much damage their pre-Christ life has done to their relationships, especially their relationships with the ones they were most meant to love. And our normal tendency to try to "fix things" (reputedly truer among men) pushes us to repair the damage quickly and cleanly. Sad to say, this may not be possible. You may be forced, in one of the hardest demands of our faith, to "wait upon the Lord." But meanwhile you can continue to pray for your own maturing process. God's work in each of us is ongoing, and we really should both desire and endeavor to "grow 'til we go," allowing him to produce increasingly Christlike traits in us until we, in our physical death, join Christ for eternity as joint-heirs of the kingdom of God. We do this best when we find ourselves more and more dependent on God's Spirit for our strength and righteousness and less and less convinced that we will succeed in his kingdom by our savvy or resolve.

Above all the traits that we would encourage you to pursue is this one: humility. True Christian humility defers first to Jesus as Lord of our lives, then defers to others in obedience to Jesus' command to "love your neighbor as yourself." Humility moves oneself out of the way so that others may see Jesus at work in us. And when it comes to loving our adult children, that very vision of Jesus is what we want for our children more than anything. For your children to see "a better you" is not enough; they must see that it is Jesus in you that is making the lasting difference. It doesn't hurt to be motivated as well by James' words: "Humble yourselves before the Lord, and he will lift you up" (James 4:10).

Finally, a word about words. Contrary to a popular axiom that actions speak louder than words, consider this: words *are* actions. They can infuriate, discourage and separate people in ways far more lasting than a roundhouse punch. However, when spoken in humility through apologies and restitutions, words can bring healing. When spoken in earnestness and honesty, complimentary words and affirming words can serve to edify (or build up) others, an act the Bible exhorts us to do for one another through both our actions (Romans 15:2) and our words (1 Thessalonians 5:11). And when spoken in love, words of correction and challenge can help to set another right. But in nearly all contexts where the Scripture presents these ideas, it is speaking of the relationships among those who believe, for in their belief the Holy Spirit guides not only their tongues but their ears as well. Godly people are of the right mind and spirit to receive the full range of rightly delivered words from other believers. Unfortunately, the same cannot be said for those who do not believe, for their spirits are resistant to God and the ways he wants us to live. For this reason, if you find yourself in a position to converse openly with your unbelieving adult children, be cautious not to erect walls made up of moral standards, even if they are biblical. Paul wrote to the Corinthians that he placed no such expectations on unbelievers because their hearts were not yet aligned by faith with Jesus (see 1 Corinthians 5:9-13).

Share Jesus and the things you have asked God to work on in your own life, then step back from your words and live your life. Let your children decide, as the Holy Spirit moves them, whether the work of God in you and others is real indeed. Don't worry about God—he'll surely prove himself!

A habit of blessing

We close this chapter by hoping to ignite you in one strong direction toward your adult children. You should look for every possible way to bless your children.

There is a hierarchy of blessings that we should hope to

maintain with our children, if our lives are truly in Christ:

1. The top priority is to see them blessed by the wondrous person and saving work of Jesus. We should "pray without ceasing" that they come to revere the Father and walk with his Son, being led by the Holy Spirit.

2. The second priority, once this first priority happens, is to see them blessed by engagement in a community of faith, where brothers and sisters in Christ support one another. In most cases, this is a local church, where grace-first preaching honors the work of the

> **The hierarchy of God's blessings for your children**
>
> **1** Blessed with salvation through Jesus
>
> **2** Blessed with a community of faith
>
> **3** Blessed with a family, if it is God's will
>
> **4** Material blessings

cross and where grace-rendering leadership disciples the believers in large and small contexts. Moreover, in this setting, we want to see our children blessed in their own spiritual growth, so that their families and businesses and recreations are touched by the Spirit of Christ in them.

3. The third priority would be the blessing of family, if God so wills this for your children. It is important for parents (often mothers most!) to recognize that God does not lead every adult into marriage and/or parenthood. Some plans of God are better enacted through single people or childless couples. That said, both the cultural histories of the Bible and the teachings of the

New Testament demonstrate that God normally does desire men and women to come together in marriage and then to raise up children "in the nurture and admonition of the Lord." Thus, there is no shame in praying for this blessing to come to your adult children. In fact, because it is increasingly common for adults to return to the church and to the Lord after their own children are born, this may be an excellent blessing to pray for your children! And mothers, if your daughters particularly confide in you that they wish to but are having trouble having children, you may make it a special point of committed prayer that she conceive—and, if you think your daughter will be willing to hear it, to actually tell her that you will make such a prayer commitment for her sake.

4. Falling below these three priorities would be material blessings, and some of the adjunct blessings that enable that: jobs and wise personal financial management, for instance. To bless your children in material ways through your own giving is partly a matter of judgment and you do want to use discretion in this regard if you think your blessings here would hinder your child's pursuit of the higher priority blessings; however, these kinds of blessings may also be a way to show that you do love your child and wish to help them "make a way" for themselves.

In the midst of all these priorities, you will need to use some of the guiding principles we have discussed earlier, including letting your life shine ahead of your words. And, especially when it comes to family matters and material provision, you will need to strike the balance between what is a blessing and what is an imposition. You may see an envelope of cash as a "gift," while your adult child may see it as a vote of no-confidence in their ability to establish independence. Check your motives and do your best to see your actions from your children's point of view—are they readily recognizing something ulterior in your actions just as you are readily ignoring it?

Still, let us encourage you in four specific ways.

The first of these needs no expounding, as we have already presented it earlier in this chapter. *Pray for your children*, especially for their salvation and their establishment in Jesus.

Second, *bless your children with information*, researching possible suggestions on your child's behalf. It may be that as a new believer or one returning to the church, they aren't motivated in finding a local fellowship or aren't sure how to choose one. Even if you live in a different locale,

> **Four ways to bless your adult children**
> - Pray for them
> - Gather information on their behalf
> - Bless your grandchildren
> - Help them materially

with the assistance of the Internet and perhaps the counsel of your own pastor, you may be able to recommend several churches to your child. Notice a key word there: several. By offering multiple options, your suggestions don't come across as a push: "You really should go here." Rather, choices allow your child to start the search and continue it on their own. (By the way, this same sort of blessing may be applied to other contexts and may be especially appreciated by a child who recognizes a need but feels overwhelmed or unequipped to find answers on their own.)

Third, *bless your children through your grandchildren*. It is true that even the best parents make mistakes with their children. How could they not? They've never been a parent before! But if our children do start families and bring grand-children into the extended family, we may find avenues for blessings our children's homes through our grandchildren, especially according to the maturing that God has done in us as time has passed from the childhood years of our children to the fresh childhood years of our grandchildren. Of course, you must keep in mind the need to respect your children as parents, adhering to their preferences regarding discipline, education, treats, etc. If they express a wish that falls outside the confines of the way you believe God would have you in-teract with your grandchildren, you may need to decline to interact with your grandchildren in these contexts. But you should also recognize that the way you interrelate with your grandchildren may be part of the "proving ground" through which God will demonstrate the work he is doing in your life. Allow him to be your guide as you consult with him in prayer, and you will see the fruit of your adherence to his direction, as opposed to going with your "best instincts" or taking a stand on somewhat incidental issues.

And fourth, go ahead and *bless your adult children materi-ally*. This may include bringing your son or daughter into the family business or helping with mortgage or auto payments. Check your heart and make sure that you are doing this in the spirit of wanting to develop and maintain a God-knit extend-ed family. In this same spirit, you may need to draw boundar-ies on your own generosity so that you do not enable laziness, mismanagement, or improper dependence in your adult chil-dren. Still, families in other cultural settings (different in time and/or place from our own) frequently weave the generations more fluidly than we do in America. As a matter of fact, I (JC) share a home with my in-laws, and I find that our family is far *more* functional because of this arrangement! You might also find that generosity is a way to reopen the lines of honest communication between you and your adult children. If you approach them by saying, "This is something we would like to do for you. However, we don't want to do this if it makes you uncomfortable or feels like an imposition." A marvelous restoring process may arise from such a conversation, as you recognize that your gift may be misinterpreted by your child and you honor their perspective on what you desire to do.

Pray more for your children and grandchildren and meditate on how the Lord would have you love and bless your children and grandchildren in "winning ways"—ways that glorify God and cause them to consider his goodness and salvation.

5 TOUGH QUESTIONS | OUR BEST ANSWERS

As you well know, parenting is almost never easy. In fact, if this book is evidence in itself, parenting may become increasingly difficult as we and our children grow older. Comparing notes with a father of grade school children recently, I (JH) laughed with him that the toughest problems always seem to happen in the middle of the night. It may start with upset stomachs and nightmares when our kids are little, but it advances to broken curfews and tearful phone calls—all when we should be sleeping!

In our conversational experience with many parents, however, we are amazed at the difficulty of circumstances that confront adult parents. No one parent has to deal with every possible trial in the world, but nearly all of us face challenges we never anticipated. We are still parents who have never parented before, and while our novice nature may be met by increasing general maturity, we still get caught in situations that test our faith and trust in God. Our children will frequently serve as the means by which God trains and purifies us, perhaps until the day we go to be with him.

In this chapter, we will lay out some of the questions and entanglements that have been presented to us by loving parents, some who find themselves in desperate circumstances. To these questions, we will offer our best answers. That is, we will lay out the wisdom that God has given us to date, by his word and by his leading. Certainly, for each scenario, there are others who would know better than we do, adding the wisdom of personal experiences that God has sovereignly taken them through. For this reason, we have established a blog for the readers of this book to come alongside us and one another and offer cross-mentoring under the Lord's covering.

You may visit it here: *loveneverfailsbook.wordpress.com*.

Fundamentally, I am reading this book because I believe that what I possess in Jesus is right and what my children have, separated from Jesus as they are, is not right. But how do I talk to them about this without sounding like I'm saying, "I'm right and you're not"?

When we and our children are all adults, the way that we best say "I'm right and you're wrong" is with our lives. The opportunities to exercise our parental authority over our children essentially vanish when they leave the structure of our home. However, a new authority arises when Jesus takes hold of our hearts. It is the same kind of authority we give to strong leaders in Jesus when we come to him—it is the authority we give them based on the respect we have because their lives align with their words.

As writers who interact frequently with men and women in country club settings, we are amazed ourselves to see the change that comes when a man, say, becomes more enamored with the ministerial work he has been given to do at a high-security prison than with his 9:15 tee time—and we're talking about lay people! Now imagine what happens when adult children see this kind of change in perspective and emphasis in their parents. While it is relatively easy to argue with a belief system that is offered up only as a list of ideas, it is hard to say to someone, "I can't accept the work you are doing to help those who need it most." Without Christ, they may in no way be compelled to engage in this work themselves, and they may for a time see it as the acts of a religious fanatic. But the more time people spend around someone who is regularly acting in faith, the more they see the authenticity that is required to keep this going. And they begin to wonder, *Is this real?*

The good news here is that while you may not have the constant access to your children that you had when they were under your roof in their youth, you may have far more leverage with them, spiritually speaking, than you have ever had. This book is written in many ways for parents who may be moving toward the end of their working lives. Generally this affords you more time—as do the decreased demands of your own household—to focus on spiritual matters: prayer, study, worship, service. If you are one who has gained much through your quiet times before the Lord, either on your own or with your spouse, consider now how you might use such times for giving. That is, pray more for your children and grandchildren and meditate on how the Lord would have you love and bless your children and grandchildren in "winning ways"—ways that glorify God and cause them to consider his goodness and salvation. If you do these things faithfully and "faith-filledly," you will find that Christ's righteousness in you speaks far more loudly than any arguments you can ever make about what is "right."

My daughter is reaping some difficult consequences because of the sinful choices she has made in her life. To what extent should

I intervene, and if I do am I sending a message that these actions were okay or even enabling my child for future destructive behavior?

Before we answer this question with regard to some lesser consequences, we want to state that there is one scenario where it is unequivocally acceptable for a parent to intervene. That is in cases where a child is being physically abused. The most common demonstration of this comes when a daughter—whether she is wayward or not in her faith—unknowingly enters a marriage with a man who begins to physically abuse her. Sometimes a parent is the first person to become aware of this scenario, and swift action is not only acceptable, it is imperative. If you do not feel equipped to enter the home and rescue your daughter yourself, then call the police, give them all the evidence of abuse you have, and pursue the matter through them until your daughter reaches a safe harbor.

Moving on…

Alcoholism, addiction and crime may all produce crippling consequences, not only personally but financially. Although parents may feel unqualified to provide the level of counseling or emotional support that their troubled adult child needs, they may find themselves in a position to offer financial help. Indeed, we know of Christian parents who have paid a high financial cost—sometimes $100,000 and more—for rehabilitation programs, legal costs of incarceration or divorce proceedings, or the cost of getting children back on their feet after they have lost everything because of sinful choices. So the question of whether or not parents should help in this way, or where they should draw the line, is an excellent one.

In Romans 11:22, we read these words: "Consider therefore the kindness and sternness of God: sternness to those who fell, but kindness to you, provided that you continue in his kindness." Some translations select the word *severity* in the place of *sternness*. Either way, we recognize that God dispenses his nature according to what we deserve from him. While he begins with the loving offer of salvation through his Son, Jesus Christ, if we reject that offer ("fall"), then we will find his severity in our path. On the other hand, if we latch onto his kindness and remain there, we will find him to be continuingly kind to us. If we are ambassadors of Christ, then, we might say that we too should demonstrate both kindness and severity to those we know best, including our children. But we must recognize our limitations. In our sinful natures, we already tend toward severity. We are nearly always more loving toward ourselves than we are toward others. And we receive God's forgiveness more readily for ourselves than we are willing to apply it to others. Therefore, we must check ourselves by striving to be as kind as possible in all situations. A parent who chooses to help an adult child out of love for God and love for the child almost always does the right thing (as opposed to parents who help a child in an attempt to assuage their own guilt perhaps). We are reminded of the remarkable story of baseball star Josh Hamilton, who left his addiction and returned to Jesus because of the care of his grandmother, who took him in when all others found it difficult to do so any more. Her hospitality and love while he was still addicted helped restore him to his Lord, his wife, his children, and his career.

It is true, however, that sometimes love for one member of a family can conflict with love for other members. For one, parents should never feel obligated to set aside their own moral confines by allowing an adult child, for instance, to break biblical sexual principles while staying in the parents' home, as this can create real strife between the parents, who are spouses protecting one another. For another, parents should never endanger other family members by hosting alongside these other family members an adult child who is known to be uncontrollably violent or who has been convicted of a crime that may be repeated (especially molestation, if children would be present). Adamant lines must be drawn for the preservation of a marriage or the extended family.

Also, it should be noted that even in their adulthood, your fairness is an important quality to maintain among your children. If you are spending large amounts of money to help a desperate child who has hurt you in many ways but are stingy with those children who have honored you and your faith, you can count on contention arising in your family relationships. Be sure to be open and encouraging and supportive of your "good children" at the same time that you are assisting those in trouble.

Before moving on, allow us to appeal to Scripture one more time, identifying our universal position—whether parents or children—in relation to Paul's words to the Romans:

> But God demonstrates his own love for us in this: While we were still sinners, Christ died for us. (Romans 5:8)

You see, to render kindness to the most needy among us—those who may not yet recognize the residence and result of their sin—is to render kindness in the same way God rendered his kindness to us. Remember, Jesus died for your sin before you were born. And his salvation waited you out, through your own years of sin. It is fitting that we love our children in this way, even if it costs us; it certainly cost Jesus to show love like this!

I am fortunate, because my children all still love us, their parents, and desire to spend time with us. However, this causes us some confusion when we consider possibilities like family vacations. We have the means and are happy to pay the way for our children who are married, but should our generosity extend to our son who is living with his girlfriend and says they have no plans to be married? Doesn't it send the wrong message to support his unrighteous choices?

This is a great question because it invites our consideration on different levels: children versus adults, believers versus non-believers, and the direction of the Holy Spirit.

We have already made it clear that when your children have left your home and their dependency on your finances, you have entered a very different season in your relationship with your children. They are truly on their own. For this reason, the messages you send may have less effect and greater consequence than they did when your children lived under your parental management, so to speak. More than that, the messages are so easily mixed. When your child is grown and gone and you reach out in love, are you doing this because she is your child (and you want to bless her) or because you are her parent (and you want to instruct her)? You see, sometimes the message we think we are clearly sending isn't so clear after all.

In a scenario involving a son who is living with his girlfriend, as this question describes, is it too much of a good thing to invite them along on a family trip, but acceptable to ask them out to a nice dinner? You may decide that neither feels right to you—and in the process you hinder the conversational relationship you desire with your son and his girlfriend.

And maybe we should stop here and ask pointedly: you do desire such a relationship, don't you? It is interesting that we will sometimes treat family members far differently than we would a friend or a neighbor. For instance, if an unmarried neighbor couple with whom you and your spouse have begun to develop a conversational relationship invites you to join them for a weekend away, how would you respond? Consider: this may be the open door you have been looking for to sit down with this couple in an unhurried setting and tell them about Jesus. And certainly this would be your prayer—that a Christian couple would jump at the opportunity to spend time with your son and his girlfriend and express to them the work that God does in our lives through Jesus. All of this must be taken into consideration—alongside the holy desires of God for our lives—when we make decisions about where and how we spend time with our children, especially if they are not believers.

There lies another critical question. When Paul wrote to the Corinthians about a loose-living believer in their midst, he told them to toss this guy out of the fellowship. The man needed to bear the consequences of his sin if he was to wise up to God's design for his life as a believer (1 Corinthians 5:1-5). But later in this same chapter, Paul wrote that he would never hold an unbeliever to the same moral standard. Clearly, there is a difference between the way we interact with believers and unbelievers when it comes to the implementation of godly righteousness. What makes this difficult for many Christian parents is that they must come to grips with the reality that their child is an unbeliever. But it matters greatly that you know whether or not your child professes to believe in Jesus. According to Paul's teaching in 1 Corinthians 5, if your child is telling his friends and family that he is a believer but living an unrepentant and ungodly life, he must be confronted, even shunned. But if he is making no such pretenses and claiming no salvation through Jesus, he must be met with mercy—the same kind of mercy that God shows us as we turn our sinful hearts to him.

Thus, it is important that we continue to grow in our own relationship with Jesus. For one thing, we want to be able to demonstrate his brand of mercy to those who need him. For another, we want to be able to increasingly discern his word and his voice for these difficult decisions we must make when interacting with our adult children. The direction of the Holy Spirit is vital if we want to rightly apply the general directives of God's word to the specific circumstances of our lives.

My Christian child is seriously dating (or engaged) to an unbeliever. What can I say that will cause my child to think twice about entering this permanent relationship?

Those who have been married will universally understand this statement: Marriage is an intimate, demanding relationship; you want to make the right choice.

That said, there may be few words you can say to your children when they are in the throes of love that will succeed in derailing their intentions. But if they are truly serious about their own commitment to Jesus, you may be able to point them to Scriptures that awaken their consideration of the seriousness of the step they are about to take. Here are a few passages that should generate this kind of thinking:

Proverbs 31:10-31. While this passage is well-known for its description of an especially godly wife, several verses point toward excellence in a husband as well. When a believer progressing toward marriage reads this passage, he or she should ask: Does my potential spouse demonstrate these characteristics and/or the desire to attain and develop them further?

1 Corinthians 7:1-4. When a believer progressing toward marriage reads this passage, he or she should ask: Is my potential spouse committed to faithfulness, and what evidence do I have of this other than a verbal promise?

2 Corinthians 4:14-15. When a believer progressing toward marriage reads this passage, he or she should ask: By marrying this unbeliever, in what ways am I uniting myself with someone whose values and ambitions are significantly different than mine?

Ephesians 5:22-33. When a believer progressing toward marriage reads this passage, he or she should ask: Is this person in any way interested in loving me according to the principles discussed here?

Yes, it is possible that a believing spouse may see his or her partner turn to Jesus (see 1 Corinthians 7 for a discussion of this matter and of the situation where a believer and an unbeliever are already married). And it is also true, if we are honest, that there is no magic formula for marriage. Some "perfect Christian marriages" end in divorce and some worldly unions last for decades until death. But God has made clear his plan for excellence in marriage, and it is difficult to see the fulfillment of his plan as a likely outcome when a believer and an unbeliever enter into marriage together. For this reason, we encourage you to initiate a conversation with your believing child (or have a trusted friend do so) about this matter.

My son claims to believe in Jesus, but he attends a church where the Bible is not accurately taught, in our opinion, and we do not trust that he and his family are in right relationship with the God of the Bible. How should we approach this?

Above all, keep in mind that as parents, we tend to steer conversations in a direction that our children anticipate negatively. If you keep coming back to the same questions and topics—*why aren't you married? when will you two be having children? do you really think the president is making the best choices for America? don't you think it would be good for you to be plugged into a church?*—your adult children will begin to dread meeting up with you. You do not even have to possess an overbearing nature for this to happen. It's just that none of us like to be confronted again and again with the differences between our position and someone else's, especially when that someone else naturally holds a condescending authority, such as a boss with an employee or a parent with a child. This is the primary reason that we wrote earlier about the habit parents should adopt of praying for people to enter their adult children's lives who would speak live-giving words (maybe the very words you would speak!) that your children hear in a way that they do not hear them from you.

Still, you do want to do some anticipating of your own. You want to anticipate that God may open the door for you to have a single powerful conversation with your children about matters as critical as the one addressed in this question. An authentic relationship with Jesus who is God is the most important need of every person, including your children and grandchildren. You should desire this for them, and you should hope to have an opportunity to present your thoughts to them about the crucial differences between what you believe and practice and what they believe and practice. However, you must keep in mind that you may get only one shot at initiating this conversation. Therefore, a second excellent prayer is to ask God to help you keep your mouth shut until you are ready to truly represent him and make a compelling case for the deity of Jesus and the vitality of following him! This does not mean that you have to become an expert in apologetics first or have every last sin weeded out of your life. But it does mean that until God opens that door of opportunity, you should be preparing for it with study and with prayer. This is especially necessary when your child is engaged in a church that teaches falsely (denying the deity of Jesus, for instance, or the saving power of his death and resurrection), for many of those churches do an outstanding job of training their people to defend what they believe.

We would do well to note too that while you may have just "one shot" at initiating this conversation, if you do it well, your children may come back to you later, wishing to continue the conversation at their own impetus. Then, for sure, you do not what to shy away from speaking more. When your children ask, they are far more ready to listen than when you start in on them without that open door.

Finally, there is a difference between a false religion and a lifeless church. Sometimes, a church may state the tenets of its belief through a creed that honors Scripture, but the people in the church are really only "checking in" on Sundays and have no personal commitment to spiritual growth. If your children are attending a church like this, they will likely be willing to attend church with you. A visit to a God-infused church where the people are vibrant in their worship and eager to study the Bible together and support one another in prayer and in sharing—assuming that is the kind of church you attend!—may well encourage them to seek such a church for the spiritual health of their own family. Likewise, you may be able to offer such comments as, "We are being encouraged and challenged by the teaching of our pastor lately. I can send you a link to his sermon if you'd like."

My children loved my parents, their grandparents. However, my parents were not believers and have passed away. Now my children accuse us of believing in a God who would send my parents to hell for their lack of faith. Frankly, I struggle with this idea myself. What can I tell my children?

This question is not specific to this situation only. Many parents who have lost wayward adult children struggle intensely with the question, "Is my child in hell?" Indeed, many have rejected the Good News of Jesus for this reason alone. So the question, while difficult, is a very good one.

We do know from Scripture that God is judge. Consider the lines of Hebrews 12:13-14, which give us a present picture of our life in God, but also of our future life in him:

> ...you have come to Mount Zion, to the city of the living God, the heavenly Jerusalem. You have come to thousands upon thousands of angels in joyful assembly, to the church of the firstborn, whose names are written in heaven. You have come to God, the Judge of all...

The emphasis is ours, confirming Scripture's claim that God is judge. He sees the lives of all men and women, and makes an assessment of the faith on which that life was built. By *faith* here, we do not mean a religious system, but rather the actual trait of believing dependence as it is applied by each person toward God: Have you believed in Jesus as Savior and demonstrated this belief by living in dependence and trust in him?

This is the kind of judge we have, one who can, does and will make this sort of assessment of our interior lives. However, he is also exclusive in this role. That is, he alone is the judge of our faith. Human judges may judge our actions, as they do in a court of law, but only God may judge the motivation of our actions as well, for only God knows our heart in a way that can see its true intent.

What this means is that we can never completely know the state of another person's account with God. The thief next to Jesus on the cross was promised paradise on the basis of his dying request to join Jesus there. Throughout history, countless people have made the same kind of eleventh hour decision to surrender to Jesus. Thus, when we say that we cannot follow Jesus ourselves because Jesus sent a beloved relative to hell, we make two grave errors. First, we establish ourselves as judge over the dead person, saying in essence that the life I saw the person live would lead me to believe that they are in hell; and because I believe this, therefore they must be in hell; so shame on God for putting them in that dreadful place! Such thinking puts us in the position of not allowing God to judge someone's faith, while permitting ourselves to do so—and to judge God in the mix. Second, when we reject the Gospel because our loved one may be in hell, we make our own eternal decision on the basis of another's story, the fullness of which we cannot know. And we do this by accepting some Scriptures—those that teach the existence of hell—while rejecting others—those that teach that God is love (Psalm 86:5, Joel 2:13, 1 John 3:16, 1 John 4:15-16).

Moreover, while many pastors and theologians are not sure how this fits into the overall system of God's judgment, Jesus told a parable in Luke 12 that suggests a proportional understanding and judgment on God's part:

> The servant who knows the master's will and does not get ready or does not do what the master wants will be beaten with many blows. But the one who does not know and does things deserving punishment will be beaten with few blows. From everyone who has been given much,

much will be demanded; and from the one who has been entrusted with much, much more will be asked.

Again, if nothing else, we should take from a passage such as this that the life about which we should be most concerned in terms of God's judgment is our own. Where do I stand with God? What is my level of responsibility? When we focus here—on ourselves—what we find is that there is only one sure way of knowing we are right in God's eyes, and that is by placing ourselves under the atoning covering of Jesus' shed blood. Without faith in Jesus and his work, we are left to our own devices, so to speak, and it is precisely our own devices that are lacking when set against the holiness of God.

Lastly, you may need to ask yourself this all-important question: *In the end, when I do stand before God, will I be the one who is revealed to be excellent in all my ways, or will he be the one who is revealed to be excellent in all his ways?* Certainly, if we believe in God at all, we must believe in a God who is over and above all his creation, including us, in knowledge and behavior and spirit. Many challengers in our time want to say, "Well, I can't believe in a God who would..." But those very words carry a strange logic—for if God is indeed there, we have no power to set ourselves above his nature and his program. To believe in a God who acts differently than we think he should is to make ourselves God above God! If that is what we do, and we do it in great error, then it is not so much God who removes us from his perfect and loving presence for all of eternity; we remove ourselves by the trajectory we have set in our refusal of him (see 2 Thessalonians 1:5-10).

Our daughter says that she is an atheist and that she can never believe in God if he allows evil in the world. Is there a way to respond to this argument?

You might begin by asking this question: *How do you recognize evil?* This question provides a helpful starting point because the recognition of evil requires a commensurate recognition of good. According to Scripture, God created men and women in his own image. This is not just a physical representation. We alone among the creatures of earth possess a spiritual component. It is that component that allows us to see good and see evil. But here's the catch. According to those same Scriptures, the ability to see evil came from humanity's rebellion against God. The tree that bore the forbidden fruit was the tree of the knowledge of good and evil. Before this rebellious act—the first sin—humanity did not see evil and did not engage in evil. Therefore, while God did allow for the possibility of evil in the world, God did not introduce evil into the world. We did. For that reason we can say that God does not enjoy the evil that has festered in our world even into our time; the enjoyment of evil is the work of humanity.

This, of course, introduces a second entangling question: *Who gets to determine what qualifies as evil?* Some people would call a cheating spouse who leaves for another lover "evil." Others would say that evil involves more than this— say, the psychological torture of the faithful spouse through false repentances followed by renewed affairs. The legal structures of most societies classify crimes as more or less evil, depending especially on whether or not they were perpetrated against minors. And culturally, some viewers would call horror movies or bloody video games themselves "evil," while others would argue that only the acts they depict, when enacted in the real world, are evil.

In other words, allowing ourselves to be the determiners of what qualifies as evil, then condemning God on the basis of our definition, doesn't just dismiss God—it replaces God with our own best thinking. And if we permit this for ourselves, then we must permit it for others—even if they call our sins "evil!"

While these lines of reasoning challenge a lack of belief because God is, in one's own eyes, evil, they do not actually answer the question of why God allows evil (or, more accurately, why God has allowed evil to continue since the sin of Adam and Eve and the murder of Abel by Cain). That question may best be answered in two parts:

(1) God allows evil because he made men and women with the ability to accept or reject him. This includes accepting or rejecting the right order of the world as he has laid it out. You may choose to obey the directives of God in Scripture, or you may not. You may choose to put your trust in Jesus, or you may not. And you always have this choice, right up to the hour of your death. You may not live for God today, but you may turn to him in another time, loving and living for him. God could wipe out evil, but if he did so, he would have to wipe out all those who have not yet turned to him. Which leads us to the second part of the answer...

(2) God allows evil because in recognizing evil, a person may correspondingly recognize their need for Jesus. When I stop quibbling over the debatable shades of evil, as discussed above, I will land in one of two spots. Either I will say that all intentional bad behavior is evil and that the God who supposedly rules the universe is impotent to contain it; or I will say that even my intentional bad behavior is evil, and I must do whatever it takes to be made right with God. If I never recognize evil to be my own condition, if I go around saying that I am doing mostly good things and so are those around me (even though one sin a day in an average life amounts to more than 25,000 sins to bring before a perfect God in the

end), then I will never turn my life over to the only one who can save me: Jesus.

It is probably best to end this discussion with an oft-forgotten parable of Jesus that supports the notion that God allows evil in his patient waiting for those are yet to turn to him. The parable, commonly referred to as the Parable of the Weeds (or Tares), is found in Matthew 13:

> Jesus told them another parable: "The kingdom of heaven is like a man who sowed good seed in his field. But while everyone was sleeping, his enemy came and sowed weeds among the wheat, and went away. When the wheat sprouted and formed heads, then the weeds also appeared.
>
> "The owner's servants came to him and said, 'Sir, didn't you sow good seed in your field? Where then did the weeds come from?'
>
> "'An enemy did this,' he replied.
>
> "The servants asked him, 'Do you want us to go and pull them up?'
>
> "'No,' he answered, 'because while you are pulling the weeds, you may uproot the wheat with them. Let both grow together until the harvest. At that time I will tell the harvesters: First collect the weeds and tie them in bundles to be burned; then gather the wheat and bring it into my barn.'"

I fear that the relationship I had with my children when they were younger has made any potential for restoration highly improbable, and I know this is my fault because of some of the things I said and did. Is there any way to get past my own guilt? Is there any hope for restoration?

Here is a strong statement: Relief from the guilt of your past actions toward your children (or anyone else) is not possible without a deep revelation of the work of Jesus on the cross. If we are incapable of forgiving ourselves on the basis of the forgiveness Jesus offers because he atoned for all our sins by shedding his blood "once for all" (Hebrews 9:26), we make ourselves incapable of offering this forgiveness to others in any faith-filled way.

This does not mean that our memories are erased. Nor does it mean that our children's memories are erased. There may be real hurt still residing in their spirit and real remorse still residing in yours. But if Jesus cannot be trusted to forgive and restore us, then there is no such thing as the Gospel. There is no Good News. We remain dead in our sins. This is no big revelation on our part; this is the argumentation of Paul to the Corinthians, when he put forth the inexchangeable necessity of Jesus' death and resurrection:

> For what I received I passed on to you as of first importance: that Christ died for our sins according to the Scriptures, that he was buried, that he was raised on the third day according to the Scriptures, and that he appeared to Cephas, and then to the Twelve. After that, he appeared to more than five hundred of the brothers and sisters at the same time, most of whom are still living, though some have fallen asleep. Then he appeared to James, then to all the apostles, and last of all he appeared to me also, as to one abnormally born...
>
> But if it is preached that Christ has been raised from the dead, how can some of you say that there is no resurrection of the dead? If there is no resurrection of the dead, then not even Christ has been raised. And if Christ has not been raised, our preaching is useless and so is

your faith. More than that, we are then found to be false witnesses about God, for we have testified about God that he raised Christ from the dead. But he did not raise him if in fact the dead are not raised. For if the dead are not raised, then Christ has not been raised either. And if Christ has not been raised, your faith is futile; you are still in your sins.

If you are having trouble with the weight of your guilt, you need to begin with a simple prayer asking God to increase your faith in the work that has been done for you and in you. There is a significant reason for this. Until your faith is compelling enough to encourage you to give yourself as "a living sacrifice, holy and pleasing to God" (Romans 12:1), your children will see the same old you. They will not see Christ in you, changing you from who you were into what he wants you to become. Beware—this is not a moral program. This is a call-and-response life that begins with Jesus' work on the cross, is caught by your faith in the efficacy and power of that work, and continues as you exercise that faith with greater and greater dependence toward a life that honors him. "We love because God first loved us" (1 John 4:19).

You may, as we said, still feel remorse. Good! Your children will need to hear of that remorse from you, as it is part of your willingness to repent (turn in a new direction). But you will only take that step of conveying your remorse and your focus on a new life in Jesus if you trust in him enough to push past the guilt. You may think that your guilt is what led you to turn to Jesus. That is part placing our faith in him, yes. But the real reason we repent, as we noted earlier in this book, is because of God's kindness (Romans 2:4). Without it, we would have seen our sin and felt our guilt but had no good place to turn. Let this same love now wash your guilt away and lead you to make the same offer of love to others, to those who need what you have received.

Of course, you may argue that you have moved past your guilt. You are ready to talk with your children and restore your relationship with them, but they are not ready; they are too hurt. And for now this may be true. While Jesus' love on the cross removes the eternal consequences of our sin, it does not remove all the temporal consequences here on earth. When Jesus brought salvation to the house of Zacchaeus the tax collector, among the man's responses was this: "If I have cheated anybody out of anything, I will pay back four times the amount" (Luke 19:8). You too may need to consider with God the reparative actions that will help win your children back. But do not allow this to be seen as "buying" their affections. If you are going to engage in material forms of repentance, then you need to make clear that you are doing this because your relationship with Jesus compels you to do this—no matter how your children respond. They may reject the offer. They may receive it but continue to stand distant from you. You can control only your own acts of love. Make them evident, and make their motivation (Jesus) evident. From there, allow God to do the work.

And in the end, we find ourselves going back to that habit of all truly loving parents: pray for your children. Pray that God captures their hearts as he has captured yours. There are many things you cannot accomplish in rebuilding your connection to your hurt children. God alone can perform the miracles necessary for complete restoration. Ask him and ask him again to do this work!

It is painful to watch your children go through a bottoming-out experience, but it may also be a sign that God is about to get your child's attention in an indelible way.

6 WHY I WRITE THESE WORDS
BY JEFFREY CRANFORD

Two things might personally qualify a person to write this book. The first comes through the experience of being a parent of adult children. Certainly "the other Jeff" has had more experience than I have in this regard, as his children are older than mine and have begun to move into adulthood. He will tell you that he has known all along that a parent's measure is only in small part based on how their children act when they are young and under their parents' roof. The greater measure is what happens when those children leave home, where one's worth is often considered in light of principles that stray far from the teachings of Scripture. Certainly Scripture itself supports this idea, for most often the "children" we see in Scripture are adults. The kings of ancient Israel and Judah were chiefly identified by whether they had followed the ways of God "as his father had done," or not.

The other way a person may be qualified to write this book comes through the experience of being an adult child who wandered away from God and endured the pain caused by his own faithless actions. Sad to say, this is my own story. And I think it will be helpful for you to know where I went in my wanderings from God and then to see how he brought me back. Almost every week that I teach and minister among my friends in Southern California, I am approached with aching questions from parents about how best to love and reach their adult children. I am only confident in answering this question because I know what God did in my own life. I know he stands as the Redeemer, the one who takes that which is worthless and makes it exceptional!

By the time I left home for college at Rice University in the early 1980s, I was pretty much done with the Bible Belt faith I had been brought up with in Texas. There was no life in it, not for me and not for the friends I hung out with. My parents had in no way misguided me, and they were committed to Jesus through and through. But I was unconvinced, and the college life offered too many "better promises" than God did at that stage of my life.

Rice should have provided me every opportunity a young man needs. It is truly "the Texas Harvard," so I was challenged academically. I have always been someone who loves to think deeply, putting together pieces of knowledge in a unified whole. I had also been recruited to play golf for Rice, so I bore that doubly honored moniker: student-athlete. But my life was going amiss. Trying to find my own way, I instead ran into disillusionment so severe that I became increasingly convinced that life was not worth living. To push these thoughts aside, I turned to alcohol, pornography, mindless television shows, and girls. In other words, I was headed down the very path that this book describes of many adult children—a path of self-direction far from the life God would have for me.

And then came that day in the grocery store when I met Scott Brister. We were in line together and he simply struck up a conversation. Nothing significant, really. But in the midst of our talking, he made note of my name and got my phone number. A few days later, he called. He presented me with an invitation to meet with him and some others at a friend's house. In all honesty, because the Rice campus is located in a part of Houston long known for its gay population, I thought this may be a sort of proposition. But I figured I could at least get a free meal out of it before telling this guy that I was not gay. As it turned out, my thinking could not have been farther from the truth! I was about to be confronted with Jesus in a way that I had never been before.

This is not to say that Scott and his friends were a bunch of "holy rollers," as we have come to call those whose Christian aroma is frankly a bit stinky. As a matter of fact Scott, who was about 15 years older than I, was at the time we met well into his career as a local attorney, eventually heading to the Texas State Supreme Court as a justice from 2003-2010. This guy was a family man with a tremendous head on his shoulders. What I saw in him and his friends was not an amped up religious expression, but rather an authenticity. They believed what they sang about and talked about. They just hung out together with Jesus in their midst, and I was forced to file the event away in the back of mind.

Not long after this dinner with his friends, Scott called me again and we began to meet regularly. He would ask me about my classes or how I was playing, but inevitably the topic of Jesus would surface. I would pepper him with questions that I thought were especially insightful or challenging, things like "What about the pygmies in Africa who have never heard of Jesus?" or "Can God create a rock so big that he can't lift it?"—typical philosophical avoidances of who God is and what he might want me to do with my life. But I asked some legitimate questions too, trying to figure out whether there was anything in this for me after all. Honestly I don't remember Scott's answers, though I'm guessing I could use some of them now in my own conversations with people. What I do remember is that Scott always seemed to care. I saw Jesus in him. He was, you might say, the precise answer to a parent's prayer that their adult child would encounter someone who will say words about Jesus that the child is willing to hear. In this case, the child was me. And yet, there was more pain ahead.

With Scott's direction, I was led to Jesus, making a beginning commitment to follow him. But the years to come would expose much inadequacy in my faith.

After college, I moved to California, where I lived with my wife. I had a job as a golf professional at one of the finest clubs in the Coachella Valley, where you will find Palm Springs, Indian Wells, La Quinta, and several other golf destination cities. If you loved golf, this was where you wanted to be. So I guess you could say that I was living the dream of a young golf pro, married to a woman he thought was just right for him.

But one day, in the midst of times that were already difficult because of some circumstances beyond my control, my wife sat me down on the couch in our little home and told me, "I'm leaving you." We had been married only a couple of years. I cried like a baby, begging her not to leave, but she packed her things, walked stoically out to the car, and drove away.

I was all alone. My wife was gone. Faced with a crisis of confidence, I found the house echoing with the nightly sounds of my own screaming and weeping. While I don't think I ever fully separated myself from Jesus, I remember lying there on the floor telling God that I did not have the remotest notion of who he was and that I didn't really trust him at all. In other words, I was back at square one, telling God that I knew nothing. At the time I thought this was the worst possible starting place. Now I realize that is where God needed to take me before I could see that my life was still being lived for me even though I said that I had given my life to him. I say this knowing that there are many parents who remain protective of their children, who do not want to see them "bottom out" like I did. It is painful to watch your children go through such an experience, but it may also be a sign that God is about to get your child's attention in an indelible way. Don't give up hope for your children, even when what you see around them are terrible circumstances.

What I came to understand about myself in those dark hours was that my whole life was built on the concept of someone I thought people would admire and accept. I was going to be "a man"—either with my wife or whatever woman would see me that way. I was going to be "a winner"—using my golf prowess to gain accolades from other good players. When it came time for me to wrestle with God, he determined to move me from the notion that I could do all these things for myself to a place of utter dependence on him. I had to fear him to gain the knowledge and wisdom I so desperately wanted (Proverbs 1:7).

In those trying days, one of my favorite Christian writers offered some words about difficulty that resonated with me so deeply; they have formed one of my "battle cries" ever since. The idea is this: The wilderness is part of God's loving plan for me. Trouble is not a breakdown in the system. God's way of doing things specifically entails shaking things up (see Matthew 10:34-36 and Hebrews 12:26). In the epic account that comprises the book of Exodus, God uses the wilderness to prepare his people for the Promised Land. Why wouldn't he do the same thing with us? Our self-preserving tendency (and sometimes our child-protecting tendency) is to ask God to alleviate the trials in our lives, to soften the circumstances that are actually designed to capture our hearts for good. As we noted in chapter three, Paul actually instructed the Corinthian believers to turn a sinful brother over to Satan "for the destruction of the flesh, so that his spirit may be saved on the day of the Lord" (1 Corinthians 5:5). That's not a scripture you hear taught very often—especially not in parenting seminars. But it describes my situation so well. I had to be stripped of every fleshly interest before God could do his grand work in me. It was when I finally came to see this clearly that I found myself moving from salvation in a momentary sense to salvation in an ongoing sense. Yes, I had prayed a prayer many years before that Jesus would save my soul, but now I was being moved to a place where he was saving my life!

God was also setting me up. In the months following my own move toward him, I met someone who was just as far gone as I had been. Her name was Laura, and she was to become my wife—the wife of my faith rather than my resolve.

When we met, Laura wanted nothing to do with God. She too had been brought up around church, but the God she knew in her own mind was a God of trappings and restrictions. She didn't need him and she didn't want him. But we began to talk. And what could I tell her except for the things I had been learning myself? God, I finally realized, was not interested in my best effort or offer. He was interested in one thing only: whether I was willing to take him up on the offer of salvation his Son had made possible through his death on the cross. This is what I told Laura, and believe it or not, her heart turned like mine had. I baptized her in the bathtub of my apartment, and we were married shortly after that. No fancy wedding this time, just a trip to the Justice of the Peace.

God had so much still to do in each of our lives. My golf personality as a mini-tour professional vacillated between anger and despair. In the midst of a bad round, in front of my wife (who was caddying for me) and my playing partners, I would utter obscenities you would have a hard time finding on cable TV! If I didn't qualify to play or missed a cut, I would storm away from the scorer's tent, slam the trunk on my clubs, and speed away from the course like a NASCAR driver. And I did this with a Christian fish affixed to the bumper of my car. Eventually, I ripped it off, telling Laura that Jesus didn't deserve to be linked in any way to me. Imagine, I was the one who had introduced my wife to Jesus—the living, loving Jesus—and this was the way I was behaving. Thankfully, I could at least read the devastation in her eyes. Here was a tender heart that had only recently said yes to Jesus, and the only picture she had of him was this anger-filled, worry-filled life I was showing her. I knew I had to change and I trusted God to change me, but it was happening so slowly, so painfully.

Beyond myself, I had my wife to think of. If she couldn't see any real change happening in me, how could she have faith for change to come in her own life? Oh, we had so much growing up to do, even though we were adults as far as the world was concerned. We were married and making our own way. Shouldn't that by itself be evidence of maturity? Knowing yourself and knowing your adult children, I think you also know the answer to that question—no! God is always working on our hearts, always drawing us closer to him. It is amazing to realize just how far sin pulls us away from God's original design for his creation. And yet when in Christ we recognize how eager we are to make life happen our own way, we concurrently come to understand how completely dependent we must be on him if we are ever going to lay real claim to his saving, sanctifying work in us. (If you are new to some of this theological language, *sanctification* is the biblical idea for the process of refining us toward holiness that God does in our hearts and minds as we increasingly surrender to him. Think transformation.)

So how did we grow? How did God restore in us the mindsets and attitudes that we would need to reflect his glory? In a word, slowly. God does work miracles, and I have seen him eradicate a specific sin from a person's life overnight. But we are all complicated people, and this sin will arise where that one wanes, if we are not focused on what God would have us focus on: him. This is what it took for Laura and me. We had to keep turning to God, exploring Scripture, seeking him in prayer, obeying him even when it was uncomfortable. And through time, God has blessed us in unbelievable ways. Perhaps most surprising is that we share our home now not only with one another, but with our three delightful daughters and with Laura's parents. God has taken two selfish people and taught us how to reach out in love just as he reached out to us. We are delighted at and in awe of what God has done in our home.

Of course, we have not resolved every issue in our lives. God is still demanding our dependence! We cannot even answer questions about how it is done, at least not if you're looking for some formula outside of letting God have his way. But I hope you see that in the midst of all our ungodly waywardness, God was devising a way for us to return to him (remember 2 Samuel 14:14?). Then he enacted that plan in our lives. From our story, I want you to increase in hope that God can do all the things we have written about in this book. May it be a hope that keeps you calling out to him on behalf of your own children.

God loves to love whole families. If the Lord has called you, urge him in prayer to hold to his promise for your children and grandchildren, that they too may come to be saved.

CONCLUSION

THIS HAS NOT BEEN a long book. Because of the myriad scenarios that can arise in modern families, most parenting books could probably be reduced to one word: pray. While the most famous parenting verse in the Bible may be Proverbs 22:6, "Start your children off in the way they should go, and even when they are old they will not turn from it," the more necessary verse may be Psalm 55:22, "Cast your cares on the LORD, and he will sustain you."

We have done our best to offer models for conversation and ideas for prayer. We have attempted to answer some questions that may relate to the very things you have experienced in your family. If we could, we would climb into our car and visit your home and sit around your table and hear the cry of your heart for your children. We would talk with you and pray with you, just as we are able to do with those we minister each week in our fellowships in California. Books are not good for that kind of thing. What they are good for is allowing a lot of people in many places to consider the wisdom of Scripture and the thoughts of others who have experienced—

and worked with those who have experienced—similar trials and joys that we have. We can share life across boundaries in a way that might not otherwise be possible.

So it is our sincere hope that this book has been a true help to you. When life seems to hand us circumstances more daunting than we want to deal with, we do well to come to one another's aid as fellow believers in Jesus, the one who saves and sustains us. We are encouraged in the book of Hebrews to keep meeting with God's people for this very reason—that we might encourage one another.

And just what kind of encouragement can we provide each other? There is nothing better for encouragement than the promises of Scripture. So we will leave you such a promise that means much to us. In the second chapter of Acts, on the Pentecost day when the Holy Spirit revealed the Good News of Jesus through the apostles in Jerusalem, Peter closed his message of salvation with these words: "Repent and be baptized, every one of you, in the name of Jesus Christ for the forgiveness of your sins. And you will receive the gift of the Holy Spirit. The promise is for you *and your children* and for all who are far off—for all whom the Lord our God will call" (Acts 2:38-39, emphasis added). It was a normal operation in the Gospels and the book of Acts for salvation to come to a household, not just an individual. God loves to love whole families. If the Lord has called you, urge him in prayer to hold to his promise for your children and grandchildren, that they too may come to be saved. It is true that you may not live to see the fullness of God's work in your family. But it is truer still that he is the eternal God, reaching across generations to complete his plan for the ages. He can be sought and he can be found.

It has probably become quite clear to you by now that this is a book directed more at you than at your children. So go for it! Go after God with all your heart and with all your soul, with all your mind and with all your strength. We think you'll like what happens when you do this—in your life and the lives of those you love.

ACKNOWLEDGEMENTS

T HE LIST OF THOSE we should thank for their help in assembling this book is probably longer than we will remember here.

First, we are grateful to our board at Links Players for allowing us the freedom to recognize the needs of the people to whom we minister so that we might write a book like this for them. Golf is really just a door to the real ministry that God gives us. In this case, that ministry includes hearing the deep love of so many parents whose hearts are broken and desiring hope in Jesus for their adult children. We hope this book has given that to them.

Second, although it can be stupidly polarizing to even mention the names of Christian leaders these days, we are deeply appreciative to those who have fed us with their writing and speaking through the years. Maybe the fact that they are such an eclectic group will keep people from bickering about one's theology over another's. These leaders include: John Piper, N.T. Wright, Paul Tripp, and Rick Joyner—the last of whom first caused Jeff Cranford to recognize the godless manipulation we referred to in chapter one.

Third, we thank our friends and family who gave this book a read in its formative stages, helping us with problems big and small, including Sylvia Cranford (Jeff's mom) and Andy Fletcher. In this same vein, Jeff Hopper would like to thank the men in his small group for their prayers as this project progressed; these guys were a real encouragement.

Finally, a huge thank you to our wives, who also read through this book and let us get away with some idealizing according to Scripture even though they know we have yet to reach all these heights ourselves. While we're being sanctified in a hundred ways, they are especially being sanctified in terms of their patience with us! Laura C and Laura H: you're the best!

NOTES

[1] Frost, Michael and Hirsch, Alan. *The Shaping of Things to Come*. Peabody, Mass.: Hendrickson Publishers, 2003; Erina, NSW: Strand, 2003. This idea threads it way through the book, but is most visible in the notion of fences and wells discussed in Chapter 3 and the Appendix.

[2] Lewis, C.S. *Mere Christianity*. San Francisco: HarperSan-Francisco, 2001. Page 113. MERE CHRISTIANITY by C.S. Lewis copyright © C.S. Lewis Pte. Ltd. 1942, 1943, 1944, 1952. Extract used by permission.

www.ingramcontent.com/pod-product-compliance
Lightning Source LLC
Chambersburg PA
CBHW071005040426
42443CB00007B/665